Augustine's *De Civitate Dei*

PETER LANG
New York · San Francisco · Bern
Frankfurt am Main · Paris · London

Dorothy F. Donnelly
and
Mark A. Sherman

Augustine's *De Civitate Dei*

An Annotated Bibliography
of Modern Criticism,
1960-1990

PETER LANG
New York · San Francisco · Bern
Frankfurt am Main · Paris · London

Library of Congress Cataloging-in-Publication Data

Donnelly, Dorothy F.
    Augustine's De civitate Dei : an annotated
bibliography of modern criticism, 1960-1990 / Dorothy F.
Donnelly and Mark A. Sherman.
        p. cm.
    1. Augustine, Saint, Bishop of Hippo. De civitate
Dei—Bibliography. I. Sherman, Mark A.   II. Title.
Z8047.7.D66   [BR65.A65]   016.239'3—dc20   91-26511
ISBN 0-8204-1607-X   CIP

Die Deutsche Bibliothek-CIP-Einheitsaufnahme

Donnelly, Dorothy F.:
Augustine's De civitate dei : an annotated bibliography of
modern criticism, 1960 - 1990 / Dorothy F. Donnelly and
Mark A. Sherman.—New York; Berlin; Bern;
Frankfurt/M.; Paris; Wien: Lang, 1991
    ISBN 0-8204-1607-X

© Peter Lang Publishing, Inc., New York 1991

Contents

Author's Note

This volume provides students and scholars of Augustine with a comprehensive annotated bibliography of critical interpretations of *De civitate Dei* that appeared in print between 1960-1990. A companion volume, *The City of God: A Collection of Modern Critical Essays*, will provide the full text of the most significant studies on *The City of God* that have been published in the twentieth-century. Its main aim is to offer a selection of important contemporary essays on *The City of God* and to provide a coherent and developing account of the various approaches to the study and interpretation of Augustine's most influential work. The second volume is scheduled to be published by Peter Lang Publishing in 1992.

D. F. D.

Preface

This reference guide includes all items directly related to studies on Augustine's *De civitate Dei* published from 1960-1990 in the United States and Canada. All critical studies that treat *De civitate Dei* in some substantial way are included: monographs, sections of books, journal articles, critical introductions to editions of *De civitate Dei*, and doctoral dissertations. Generally excluded from the reference guide are studies that provide only standard information on *De civitate Dei* and works that merely mention *De civitate Dei* within the context of general studies of the history of Christian doctrine, medieval thought, the Middle Ages, and the like. Thus, the guide does not include standard encyclopedia entries, sections of works which merely discuss Augustine and his works in relation to the social and political environment of his age, journal articles that make only passing reference to *De civitate Dei*, reviews of editions of *De civitate Dei*, and general histories of theological, political, and philosophical thought. The result is a reference guide for Augustinian scholarship from 1960-1990 that includes those significant critical works directly related to the study of *De civitate Dei*. The annotations indicate the way in which each work contributes to a fuller understanding and interpretation of Augustine's text.

The work also includes two sections which supplement the main bibliography. The first is an annotated list of selected studies published in English by foreign publishers and which appeared in print between 1960-1990. The second cites selected works published prior to 1960. These sections include works that fall outside the limits that have been established but which should be included because they offer a significant contribution to the study of *De civitate Dei*. Finally, a selected bibliography of general studies on Augustine and his works is also provided. There is an immense bibliography on Augustine. Other bibliographic sources are therefore included among the citations in the general bibliography.

The growing scholarly interest in Augustine, and especially the significant increase in studies on *De civitate Dei* — by philosophers, theologians, political theorists, literary critics, and many other scholars — has generated a strong need for a comprehensive and annotated bibliography of scholarly works devoted to a study of *De civitate Dei*, perhaps the most influential work written by Augustine. There is at present no comprehensive bibliography of Augustine scholarship that is compiled and published in the United States. And there has been no annotated bibliography published of studies devoted exclusively to *De civitate Dei*. There is a special need among American scholars for a comprehensive annotated bibliography of the scholarship on *De civitate Dei* that has appeared in print in the United States and Canada in recent years. The purpose of this reference guide is to fill that need. The guide will, of course, make the works of American and Canadian scholars more accessible to Augustine scholars in other countries as well.

Acknowledgments

It is a pleasure to thank those individuals and institutions who have helped me in the preparation of this book. First and foremost among those to whom I am indebted is my Research Associate and co-author, Mark A. Sherman. Dr. Sherman and I worked on this project together while he was a doctoral candidate at the University of Rhode Island. I am indebted to him for the significant contribution he made to the preparation of this book. It is the fruit of his labors as well as of mine.

I would like to thank the entire staff at the University of Rhode Island Library (Providence Campus)—especially Jean Sheridan, Bernice Mellen, Pauline Moulson, Lorraine Bliss, and Marilyn Jamgochian—for their assistance in the research on the project. Special appreciation goes to Bernice Mellen for her work in obtaining copies of obscure and elusive items through interlibrary loan. I also want to acknowledge the invaluable help I received from Jean Sheridan, Head Librarian, particularly in the early stages of the project, in conducting computer searches to identify items relevant to the reference guide. I must express my sincere gratitude to Ethel Thompson for her outstanding work in the typing and preparation of the manuscript.

I wish to thank John M. Quinn, O.S.A., Associate Director, and Joseph C. Schnaubelt, O.S.A., Director, Augustinian Historical Institute, Villanova University. I am grateful to them for the encouragement and support they gave me in the course of working on this project. Finally, I am pleased to acknowledge that the publication of this book was assisted by a grant-in-aid from the University of Rhode Island Council on Research and an award from the URI Alumni Association Faculty Support Fund.

Dorothy F. Donnelly

Chronology

A.D.

Part I

Writings About *De civitate Dei*, 1960-1990

1 — **Adams, Jeremy D.** *The Populus of Augustine and Jerome: A Study in the Patristic Sense of Community.* **New Haven: Yale University Press, 1971.**

This study systematically examines the meanings of *populus* in Augustine's writings with special focus on its usage in *The City of God*. Consideration is also given to other words used by Augustine when discussing social and political bodies: *civitas, societas, res publica, gens, plebs*, and *regnum*. The method used by the author is to cite the frequency of the appearance of the word *populus*; identify the general patterns of its usage; discuss the attributes or properties of the word as it is used in different contexts; and analyze the distinctions between the meaning of *populus* and the other "social and political" terms used by Augustine.

The aim of this examination is to explore the "patristic sense of community." Tentative answers are sought to three principal questions: "Into which and what sorts of groups was mankind divided in the minds of patristic and early medieval thinkers? To which of those groups did they feel that they . . . belonged? If they felt a sense of community with several groups or kinds of groups, what did they feel about the proper hierarchy of loyalties in that regard?" The study argues that throughout Augustine's many writings his meaning of the term *populus* is consistent with his use of it in *The City of God*. When we take the whole range of his works together, "they permit us to see that that noun represents in Augustine's writings a fairly coherent notion, which the socio-political terminology of this century would describe as a legitimate polity, unified by an essentially conscious agreement."

The work has five appendices, two of which deal with *The City of God*. Appendix A: "Augustine's Definitions of *Populus* and the Value of Civil Society"; and Appendix B: "Content-Analysis Tables for *Populus* in *The City of God* and *Gens* in Books XV-XVIII." See Marshall, entry number 73 below.

2 — **Allen, David W.** *The Doctrine of Augustine on the Resurrection of the Dead in* **The City of God. Dissertation. Temple University, 1964.**

This study is concerned with an analysis of the doctrine of the resurrection of the dead as it occurs in *The City of God*. The final chapter of the work presents a brief survey of Jewish literature — the Old and New Testaments and the Extra-Biblical writings. The second chapter discusses the doctrine as it was taught to the church Fathers prior to the time of Augustine. The author's purpose is to show, on the one hand, that the doctrine of the resurrection of the body is of extreme importance to Augustine and, on the other, that he felt that this doctrine needed defense. It is concluded that Augustine "ably defended bodily resurrection against those who taught that all matter was evil and can have no future; and because the body is matter, it too must be set aside permanently. He also withstood the adjudged heresies of Origen and his theories of the new body."

3 — **Barnes, T. D.** "Aspects of the Background of *The City of God*." *Revue de L'universite D'Ottawa* **52 (1982), 64-80.**

As its title indicates, this article seeks to contribute to a "better understanding of the background, both historical and intellectual, against which Augustine wrote *The City of God*." The first section of the paper presents a brief overview of the contents of *The City of God*. The author notes that Augustine did not invent the idea of interpreting history in terms of two cities and proposes that he would have written a *City of God* even if Alaric had not sacked Rome. Yet, "*The City of God* which he did write has been deeply influenced, in both form and content, by the historical circumstances of its composition." The main portion of the study is devoted to a discussion of a number of social, political, and religious "circumstances" which influenced the particular character of *The City of God* and, at the same time, cites specific passages from the text where Augustine responds to these contemporary events and opinions.

4 — Barr, Robert R. "The Two Cities in Saint Augustine." *Laval theologique et philosophique* **18 (1962), 211-229.**

By an extended summary review of passages in *De civitate Dei* and modern critical opinion of the work this article serves as a primer to Augustine's idea of the "two cities." The author briefly examines the relationship of *De civitate Dei* to the utopian ideal and then turns to the subject of history in *De civitate Dei* and, conversely, the influence of the work itself in history—medieval, particularly. The central issues discussed in the essay are the natures and ends of Augustine's two cities, their correlation to church and state, and the critical concepts of representation and identification pertaining to those relationships. The study proposes that Augustine "never intended his City of God as anything but the mystical union of the good people of all nations." The understanding that the City of God is an accomplished fact—something real at this moment, and not some utopia elaborated as the last goal for political and social progress—would have forestalled attempts at its artificial realization in a purely temporal and political human society.

5 — Bathory, Peter Dennis. *Political Theory as Public Confession: The Social and Political Thought of St. Augustine of Hippo.* **New Brunswick: Transaction, 1981.**

The final four of nine chapters in this book comprise Part III, "The City of God: Of Foundations and Renewals." The book's thesis culminates here by connecting within Augustine's cosmic vision the personal philosophy of the *Confessions* with the political ideas in *The City of God*. The author's intent is to analyze Augustine, the man and his philosophy, within a theological and political context. The analysis of Augustine is primarily a psychological one conducted with "a sensitivity to his personal experience and memories."

Augustine's concern with education and the role of political leadership are the basis for this review of *The City of God*. Augustine's reassessment of history and belief in the educability of the average citizen coalesce into what is viewed as a progression of "leadership triads," consisting of *conditor, magister,* and *rex,* in Augustine's politico-philosophical exegesis. The author follows this method of Augustine's throughout *The City of God* in an effort to illustrate his transition from a personal "therapist of self-examination" in the *Confessions* to a "civic or political therapist" in *De civitate Dei.*

"The church," according to this essay, "became for Augustine, very much a part of the *saeculum* — of 'the world of men and of time.' " Thus his intent was to present Christianity in such a way that it could be seen within a historical as well as universal framework and subsequently be embraced as an alternative to Roman political leadership. Augustine's commentary on the origins of societies is fundamental here. Rome, founded in the violence of Romulus, was necessarily maintained by deception. A society so dependent on the *libido dominandi* would ultimately "return to principles that had over time both contributed and subverted social cohesion and order." Interwoven with this is the false ideal of the Roman hero as *magister.*

Augustine's alternative is the Old Testament patriarchy which, in its covenant with God, had leaders who could offer a temporal vision to the society in crisis and thus reaffirm the mutual love from which it was created. The second part of God's covenant with Abraham is of course Christ and the society of his founding. Through Christian self-awareness and self-confrontation on both individual and societal levels, then, a society grounded in mutual assent could, in Augustine's eyes, organize itself in a positive manner and confront common problems with a clearer sense of that which they shared. The essay stresses that this is "surely a reversal of the normal approach to Augustine that emphasizes . . . sinful man in the need of the restrictions of government." In such a society, the study notes, *auctoritas* is *libertas.*

6 — Bigongiari, Dino. "The Political Ideas of St. Augustine." In
**   *The Political Writings of St. Augustine*. Ed. Henry Paolucci.**
**   Chicago: Regnery, 1962.**

This essay offers a general overview and interpretation of the
political aspects of the *De civitate Dei*. It proposes that all of
Augustine's social and political views are connected to his theory of
predestination. Augustine's political pessimism, as articulated in
his doctrine of predestination, is traced back to pagan antiquity.
Lucian, it is noted, believed that human beings strive to fulfill all
their desires and that they are constitutionally "incapable of acting
justly."

The author observes that for Augustine, too, human beings have
an "unquenchable desire for goods." It is their self-seeking nature,
the self-seeking that Augustine calls *cupiditas*, which moves people
to form political communities. From this perspective, the state is
needed because coercion is needed. On this particular point, the
essay concludes that those who are "predestined to be saved . . .
stay in the midst of this city of the devil, as foreigners, *peregrini*,
viatori, until they are called to their true home."

Other themes briefly touched upon include Augustine's theory
of a just war, the use of force in matters of faith, and his views on
the relation between providence and history. According to the
author, "Aristotle had established that there is teleology or purpose not only in volitional acts of man but also in nature. . . .
Augustine opened the sphere of history to teleology." In sum,
there is, for Augustine, a design, a purpose, a divine plan, in the
course of human affairs.

7 — Black, Jonathan. "*De Civitate Dei* and the Commentaries of
**   Gregory the Great, Isidore, Bede, and Hrabanus Maurus**
**   on the Book of Samuel." *Augustinian Studies* 15 (1984),**
**   114-127.**

This study examines the textual use of *De civitate Dei* in four
medieval works—the commentaries of Gregory the Great
(*Expositiones in Librum Primum Regum*), Isidore of Seville
(*Quaestiones in Vetus Testamentum*), Bede (*In Primam Partem
Samuhelis Libri IV*) and Hrabanus Maurus (*Commentaria in Libros*

IV Regum). The purpose of the author's examination is to determine whether and to what extent Augustine's themes are developed in these medieval biblical commentaries.

By means of a close textual analysis of the works, the author shows where and how the *De civitate Dei* is used by these four scriptural commentators, each of whom has a different purpose. It is argued that Isidore chooses not to incorporate the "complex network of interpretations" that go into Augustine's understanding of the Old Testament. Rather, he focuses on "Augustine's commentary on the Book of Samuel prophecies, and to these he adds figurative interpretations of Old Testament events." In contrast, Bede incorporates the "full breadth of Augustine's interpretations" by use of a detailed investigation on the literal level of Augustine's commentary on the Book of Samuel. This approach, it is suggested, enhances Augustine's figurative interpretation.

Hrabanus' commentary, which makes the greatest use of Augustine's text, is, according to the author, "much less successful." The problem with Hrabanus' approach, the author argues, is that he offers interpretations "on any level for each scriptural passage." Consequently, his omissions are "severe ones," his conclusions about Augustine are often contradictory because they are rendered in such minute detail, and in many instances Augustine's meaning is lost because his views are "taken out of their thematic context."

Of the four commentators, Gregory alone does not use the *De civitate Dei*. The author suggests that Gregory did not have Augustine's work available to him when he wrote his commentary. However, the essay argues that even if Gregory had had the *De civitate Dei* available, given his purpose, he would not have had "any reason" to quote Augustine. According to the essay, the unity of the levels on which Gregory interpreted the Book of Samuel would have been destroyed had he attempted to incorporate Augustine's themes.

8 — Boler, John. "Augustine and Political Theory." *Mediaevalia: A Journal of Medieval Studies* **4 (1978), 83-97.**

This essay encourages a view of Augustine's political theory which is allied with "neither the pessimist nor the triumphalist interpretation." Indeed, from an initial suggestion that "Augustine has no political theory at all," this study investigates the possibility that, as opposed to an actual political theory, Augustine's writings and ideas embody a "species of 'political positivism' " promoting obedience and order while offering no particular scheme for the structure of the state.

To explicate this view the author first presents "in an idiosyncratic way" several political themes and passages in Augustine, in particular: order, peace, domination, justice, and revolution. This is followed by an examination of the relationship of the state to philosophical idealism. The discussion here pays close attention to the shift in Augustine's belief, precipitated by the Donatists, on the use of state force to suppress heresy and schism.

The third section of the essay deals with Augustine's thoughts on government and the most influential secular attitudes affecting his attitude, for example, the Platonic double standard on the responsibilities of ruler and ruled, and the necessarily evil nature of any political structure scrutinized in the light of perfectionism. Despite his pleas for order in temporal society, Augustine's overriding religious belief, the author says, "did not offer Christians any hope for or encouragement towards establishing a political program for the betterment of man."

Finally, in an effort to put some of his preceding points into perspective, the author notes that Augustine's intent is "not to make government more humane but to make it less necessary" by eschewing a society in which individuals assert their own rights and substituting in its place a society in which they "try to excel one another in love." Thus, what might be considered a political theory in one respect is actually apoliticism.

9 — Bourke, Vernon J. *"The City of God and the Christian View of History."* *Melanges a la Memorie de Charles De Koninck.* Quebec: Les Presses de l'Universite Laval, 1968. Pp. 69-80. Rpt. in *Wisdom from St. Augustine.* Houston: The Center for Thomistic Studies, 1984. Pp. 188-205.

The author discusses *The City of God* from the perspective of the philosophy of history it presents. He points out that Augustine is "completely theocentric in his thinking" and his interpretation of human events is consistently informed by this attitude. For Augustine, the essay argues, human history, of itself, has no ultimate meaning or significance. Temporal history is given meaning only through divine providence, and the events of this world are explainable only within the context of the concepts of redemption and salvation. The study concludes that Augustine's primary purpose in writing *The City of God* was to articulate a fully developed Christian view of history.

The essay also briefly contrasts Augustine's view of history with that of Thomas Aquinas. It is pointed out that Aquinas often speaks of a *communicatio divina* and of the *regnum Dei*. But he does not, it is argued, develop a theory of history, nor does he propose that divine providence is manifested in the temporal world. Unlike Augustine, in Thomas Aquinas's view, according to the author, "history is a mere chronicle of events."

10 — Brawer, Robert A. "St. Augustine's Two Cities as Medieval Dramatic Exempla." *Mediaevalia: A Journal of Mediaeval Studies* 4 (1978), 225-244.

Through an examination of three of the Townley Corpus Christi plays this study discovers a systematic presentation of a theological view of history similar to that in Augustine's *The City of God*. And as in *The City of God*, the representation of historical events in the Corpus Christi plays is secondary to the elucidation of moral and spiritual choices. The idea of the two cities provides a polarized theological construct for dramatizing the choice human beings have in this life between divine harmony and earthly discord. "Of all the works in the Middle Ages that represent the Augustinian concept of discord and accord, only the cycle drama does so in other than absolute terms." Following Augustine, there is in the Corpus Christi plays an implicit recognition of degrees of goodness in the individual's progress from being a sojourner in the *civitas terrena* to being a citizen of the *civitas Dei*.

Thomas of India, the *Second Shepherds' Play*, and the trial and crucifixion scenes of the Townley cycle are chosen to support the author's theses. The character of the doubting Thomas is seen as an exemplum of the triumph of faith; the sheep-stealer Mak is "a universal symbol of discord" who forces the shepherds to affirm their communality; the earthly tyrant Pilate, in his duplicity, is a negative exemplum "most inimical to the kind of Christian commonwealth that is an earthly paradigm of heaven's peace."

The author also emphasizes the didactic element in the Townley Plays and points out that such performances were intended to "perfect the faith of the audience, to move it . . . toward a personal and communal integrity characteristic of 'heuen citee.' "

11 — Brown, Peter. *Augustine of Hippo: A Biography.* **California: University of California Press, 1967.**

Chapters 26 and 27 of this extended study of Augustine's life and writings offer a comprehensive summary and discussion of the main ideas and principal themes presented by Augustine in *De civitate Dei.*

In Chapter 26 ("*Opus magnum et arduum*: Writing the 'City of God' "), the author offers a general overview of the historical and personal circumstances which gave rise to Augustine's writing of *The City of God.* The author says that "*The City of God* is the last round in a long drama: written by a former protégé of Symmachus, it was to be a definitive rejection of the paganism of an aristocracy that had claimed to dominate the intellectual life of their age."

Chapter 27 ("*Civitas Peregrina*") notes that *The City of God* uses a theme that had already become a commonplace among African Christians, namely, the idea that "since the Fall of Adam, the human race had always been divided into two great pyramids of loyalty. The one 'city' served God along with His loyal angels; the other served the rebel angels, the Devil and his demons." Augustine's intention in *The City of God* is to demonstrate that a division between an earthly and a heavenly city could be seen throughout the history of the human race. It is pointed out that the *civitas terrena* "has to make room for a group of people who must remain aware of being different, for a *civitas . . . peregrina*; for resident strangers." *The City of God*, in other words, is a book about being other-worldly in this world.

12 — Brown, P. R. L. "Saint Augustine." In *Trends in Medieval Political Thought*. Ed. Beryl Smalley. Oxford: Basil Blackwell, 1965. Pp. 1-21. Rpt. as "Political Society." In *Augustine: A Collection of Critical Essays*. Ed. Robert A. Markus. New York: Doubleday, 1972. Pp. 311-335.

This essay begins with the observation that classical political theory was based upon a rational myth of the state. In contrast, modern political thought, like medieval thought, proposes that the link between the individual and the state cannot be limited merely to a rational obligation. Political society does not exist as an "extrapolated, isolated ideal"; on the contrary, it exists concretely whether the primal cause is God or history. The essay proposes that medieval as well as modern thinkers are thus indebted to Augustine for signaling the end of the concept of political idealism embedded in Greek political philosophy and substituting for it an emphasis on the basic questions that deal with the "intractable reality" of the human situation.

The main topic developed here is the notion that for Augustine rational control over one's political environment is very much limited. Augustinian political thought centers around problems of the individual's behavior in a political community. Human beings are not "natural political animals"; they are individuals faced with a whole range of aims and concerns, only some of which stem from living in political society. Augustine's political theory, according to the author, "is based upon the assumption that political activity is merely symptomatic: it is merely one way in which men express orientations that lie far deeper in themselves. . . . The symptoms which tend to predominate in his description of human political activity can only be thought of as symptoms of a disease. . . . The most blatant symptom . . . is the inversion of the harmonious order established by God."

The essay concludes by noting that for Augustine the most striking feature of life in this *saeculum* is that it is destined to be incomplete. "No human potentiality can ever reach its fulfillment in it; no human tension can ever be fully resolved." Thus although Augustine wrote approximately 117 books, none deals with political theory. Even his extensive reflections on political society, as they appear in *The City of God*, "are no more than the anxious questioning of a shadow; they are a hint of a full peace and of a full realization of hidden loves, in the Heavenly Jerusalem."

13 — Brown, Robert F. "The First Evil Will Must Be Incomprehensible: A Critique of Augustine." *Journal of the American Academy of Religion* **46 (1978), 315-329.**

This study argues that although Augustine occasionally acknowledges that an absolute origin of evil, arising from the free will of a creature, is incomprehensible, he nevertheless attempts in a number of passages in *The City of God* to give a causal account of the fall of Adam and/or Satan. The essay claims that this "conceptual blunder" leads Augustine to offer three unacceptable explanations of the fall which conflict variously with his own doctrines of divine omnipotence, the goodness of creation, and creaturely free will and responsibility.

First, his contention that free creatures made "out of nothing" inevitably fall makes the fall seem ontologically necessary (unfree) and thereby lays the ultimate responsibility for it on the Creator. Second, the appeal to pride as an explanation is a spurious causal account, for "pride" is only a synonym for "fallenness" itself and not a possible antecedent condition in a being created good and not yet fallen. Finally, Augustine's assertion that the first sin is intrinsically comprehensible, but not comprehensible to us because we are fallen, is viewed by the author as "an obfuscation masquerading as an explanation." Instead of seeking causal explanation Augustine should have stayed with his own wiser observation that an evil will has no efficient cause.

The concluding section of this paper draws upon Paul Ricoeur's study, *The Symbolism of Evil*, to argue that the narrative structure of the "Adamic" myth begets as an unfortunate by-product this tendency to spin out a causal account of the first evil. The author agrees with Ricoeur's view that the "Adamic" myth, "properly interpreted, presents a possible structure for interpreting one's present existence rather than providing a quasi-historical account of how a 'very first sin' happened."

14 — Chestnut, Glenn F. "The Pattern of the Past: Augustine's Debate With Eusebius and Sallust." In *Our Common History as Christians: Essays in Honor of Albert C. Outler*. Ed. John Deschner, et al. New York: Oxford Univ. Press, 1975. Pp. 69-95.

The author begins by suggesting that in order to better understand the significance of what Augustine says in *The City of God* we need to know two positions he particularly opposed — on the one hand, the conservative, pessimistic theories of the Roman historian Sallust and, on the other, the liberal, rationalistic optimism of Eusebius of Caesarea. Augustine rejected the ideas of these two influential thinkers and proposed a new explanation of history which he embodied in his doctrine of the two cities. According to the author, Augustine argues, unlike Sallust and Eusebius, that "history has no complete solution in this world, . . . and that it is lived in perpetual tension."

The essay offers a detailed summary of the ideas presented by Eusebius in his *Church History*, a work which the author describes as "the first full-length narrative history written from a Christian perspective." Eusebius' theology of history embraces the notion that "souls pre-existed before this earth was even created." Eusebius further proposed that in the "first primitive centuries" of human history, there existed a group called the "Friends of God" who were "Christian in fact, if not in name"; that the history of salvation involved a "gradual evolution, over long eras of history, of progressively better integrated and more humane social institutions"; and that the "divine Logos was the agent whereby the human race was lifted out of savagery and superstition, and was gradually, over the centuries, led to civilization and a rational religion."

Augustine's *The City of God*, written nearly a century after Eusebius' *Church History*, challenges the central ideas of Eusebius' theology of history. The notion of the pre-existence of the soul was rejected by Augustine in favor of the doctrine of original sin. In place of Eusebius' concept of the divine Logos he offers the doctrine of the Trinity. And for the Eusebian notion of progress Augustine substitutes the concept of two cities that were founded by two loves and which co-exist in human history. The radical difference between Eusebius and Augustine is summed up by the author this way: for Eusebius providence is empirically observable in history ("an objective pattern in the *external* course of events"); for Augustine the true significance of providence is in the personal history of the individual ("in the *inner* history of each human subject involved in the course of events").

The other important thinker with whom Augustine debates in *The City of God* is Sallust. It is stated that in his works of history Sallust claims that Rome was made great by the "thirst for glory (*cupido gloriae*) that had filled men's minds"; the sin of *ambitio*, which was "the attempt to win glory by craft and deception," brought on its decline and fall. According to the author, the cynicism of Sallust's comments on human motivation is mirrored almost exactly in Augustine's doctrine of original sin. However, in contrast to Sallust, Augustine proposes that Rome fell because its people sought glory according to the "righteousness of men rather than according to the righteousness of God."

The essay concludes that for Augustine the basis of human psychology was not simply the desire for human praise but, rather, that "love which had to be directed toward something." Augustine thus rejects Sallust's argument of a golden era in Rome's past. A true people, according to Augustine, directs its love not toward human glory but toward God, "who stands above human history . . . and who can never be threatened by the vicissitudes of purely human events."

15 — Cranz, F. Edward. *"De Civitate Dei,* **XV, 2, and Augustine's Idea of the Christian Society."** In *Augustine: A Collection of Critical Essays.* **Ed. Robert A. Markus. New York: Doubleday, 1972. Pp. 404-421. Originally in** *Speculum* **25 (1950), 215-225.**

The problem considered in this work is that while Augustine "tells us a great deal about [the City of God], he does not define it." The author speculates that one reason for this may be that for Augustine "the City of God, like grace, is so bound up with the Christian experience that it hardly admits of definition." The author suggests that part of the difficulty for modern readers in interpreting the character of Christian society in *De civitate Dei,* and in finding solutions to such problems as the relationship between "church" and "state," stems from a semantic gap between the fifth and twentieth centuries. However, if specifics about the City of God are to be found they are in Book XV, chapter 2.

In direct response to the (Neo-) Platonic interpretation given in 1925 by Hans Leisengang (i.e., a tripartite hierarchy: *civitas caelestis spiritalis, civitas terrena spiritalis, civitas terrena carnalis*), this essay suggests "a simpler, more literal exegesis." The author proposes, by analysis of Augustine's use of the word *ecclesia*, that Christian society in the temporal world is a mixture of all three groups, good or bad. Yet "there is always a sharp contrast between the present earthly mode of the Christian society and its final glory."

To develop his argument more clearly the author contrasts the ideas of Augustine with those of Eusebius of Caesarea who saw "a unified Christian empire as the goal of all history," consummated in the monarchy of Constantine. "As against the Augustinian distinction within human society between earthly and heavenly cities, earthly and heavenly kingdoms, Eusebius can say that the city of earth has become the city of God and that the monarchy of Constantine brings the kingdom of God to men." The conclusions of both thinkers originate from a single dilemma in the early social condition of Christianity, that is, its opposition to Rome. The general conversion of Rome, however, seems to have prompted drastically different responses. The author also notes that the concept of the "state" was the product of late medieval thought and is a form of thought "which neither Augustine nor Eusebius knows."

16 — Donnelly, Dorothy F.   *"The City of God* and Utopia: A Revaluation." *Augustinian Studies* **8 (1977), 111-123.**

This study considers the relationship between *The City of God* and the utopian mode of thought. The article begins with a comprehensive survey of contemporary critical opinion on utopias and utopian thought to demonstrate that the term utopia has become so all-inclusive that it is now applied to any work containing elements of what is called utopian thought; that is, "any social, intellectual, political, religious, or psychological theory that speculates about the possibilities of achieving the good life in the future." In several of the studies mentioned, *The City of God* is cited as an example of a utopian work and interpreted from this point of view.

The article argues, however, that utopia and *The City of God* are based upon significantly different underlying assumptions and premises, and they inevitably offer contrasting views on the value of the temporal world and conflicting ideas about an ideal *telos*. The work attempts to show this opposition through an analysis of four aspects of Augustine's work: his use of the term "city"; his ideas on the relationship between the individual and the state; his concept of time; and his views on and description of an "ideal existence." The study concludes that not only is *The City of God* not an example of utopian writing, but it may even be regarded as both a rejection of the utopian mode of thought and a mandate against utopianizing.

17 — Dougherty, James. "The Sacred City and *The City of God*." *Augustinian Studies* **10 (1979), 81-90.**

The idea of a sacred city was not an innovation of Augustine's, yet his concept of the City of God differed greatly from others. This essay examines how *The City of God* employs this ancient tradition and, at the same time, radically departs from it. Concurrent with the sanctification of physical space is the formation of a body politic within that space. The author illustrates the nature of the shift from the Roman *urbs* to a Christian *civitas* that was achieved by Augustine.

Fundamental to the sacred city is the notion that it constitutes a well-ordered cosmos within its bounds while all without is chaos. Rome extended this concept beyond the city walls to the far reaches of its jurisdiction. Alaric's sack of Rome in 410 violated the holy space of the city and not only prompted Augustine to write *The City of God* but afforded him the perfect metaphor as well.

According to the article, Augustine "recognized as his true adversary the still-current myth of the sacred city, and indeed the whole idea that sacredness depends on some magical arrangement of space." Augustine inverts the sacred city image through his depiction in the first ten books of *De civitate Dei* of Rome as possessed by "the very demons whom the city was supposed to exclude from its sacred ground."

The essay shows that Augustine linked the image of a sacred physical city with the Church and thereby removed the city from its role as the singular source of the *civitas*. To achieve this Augustine utilized an "ambiguous denotation of *civitas* [embracing both the] spiritual and physical," which he "complemented" with the idea of "*ecclesia*, at once the assembly of the faithful and the place of the assembly." For Augustine the Church is a "*civitas peregrina* [community in exile] dwelling in the midst of the earthly city." The article concludes that the final subordination of the physical city is seen in Augustine's view of the destiny of the *civitas Dei*. Though the Romans saw the perfection of the earthly empire, its law, and its citizens, as ultimate, Augustine insists upon the term *peregrini* for the Christian faithful. The *civitas Dei* on earth, then, is composed of members who share a communal destiny which lies beyond the bounds of historical time and the temporal world.

18 — Dougherty, Richard J. "Christian and Citizen: The Tension in St. Augustine's *De Civitate Dei*." In *Collectanea Augustiniana*. Ed. Joseph C. Schnaubelt, O.S.A. and Frederick VanFleteren. New York: Peter Lang, 1990. Pp. 205-224.

This study notes that Augustine's turn from the political to the trans-political was an inevitable outcome of his views on the ends of the state on the one hand, and civil society on the other. The tension the author studies is that which results from the coercive exercise of civil authority and the proper orientation of the Christian as citizen. It is pointed out that the human condition is distinguished in terms of two kinds of love—the citizens of the City of God love God; the citizens of the City of Man are bound by the love of earthly things. And this is the reason why there is no good "gained from political society—it aims at a love of what is perishable, while the Christian is to aim at the love of what is eternal." Yet, because the state is able to create conditions leading to earthly peace, the good person can and must make use of "earthly things." In sum, the individual's need to participate in and make use of a "political" realm, an earthly polity, conflict with the desire to focus not on human concerns but, rather, on the concerns of

God. As the author says, "a proper balance is what must be established, the balance between the concerns for the earthly good and that which takes the Christian closer to eternal destiny."

19 — Downey, Glanville. "The Ethical City, the Secular City, and the City of God." *Anglican Theological Review* 56 (1974), 34-41.

This article discusses the concept of city in Plato's *Republic*, Aristotle's *Politics*, and Augustine's *The City of God*. It is noted that Plato and Aristotle lived in the world of the *polis*, the classical Greek city that was at the same time an independent political unit. Augustine lived in the Roman empire in which pagans and Christians found themselves living side by side. Although Aristotle and Augustine represented different spiritual and intellectual traditions, they nevertheless "perceived the same dangers, and the same potential for good, behind the failures and the problems of their cities. Their insights are strikingly 'modern.' "

Aristotle, a "pragmatic observer," and Augustine, a "political realist," came to the same insight, namely, that "an understanding of the reason why the Greek *polis*, or Roman *civitas*, has come into existence will show what its nature is." Thus for both Aristotle and Augustine the human community is viewed as a "living organism" which exists and acts for a certain end. The essay observes that at the beginning of the *Politics* Aristotle announces that the basis of his study is that the *polis* is a "specific kind of *koinonia*, an association or partnership, which exists for some good." Similarly, Augustine's two cities exist for their own good, that is, for their own "certain end." The author also discusses the differences between Aristotle's and Augustine's views on the city but asserts that these differences themselves contribute to an understanding of the similarities between the views of the two thinkers.

20 — Ferrari, Leo C. "Background to Augustine's *City of God*." *The Classical Journal* 67 (1972), 198-208.

The historical situation which produced *The City of God* is the concern of this essay. From the victory of Constantine over Maxentius at Mulvian Ridge in 312 the author chronicles the spread of

Christianity over the pagan Roman Empire. Considerable attention is given to the political and ecclesiastical power of St. Ambrose as well as his influence on the young Augustine. The remainder of the article is concerned with Augustine's career, his conversion, and the composition of *The City of God* in an attempt to render futile identification of the city of Rome with the City of God.

21 — **Fortin, Ernest L.** *Political Idealism and Christianity in the Thought of St. Augustine.* **Pennsylvania: Villanova University Press, 1972.**

This work suggests that in "*The City of God* more than in any other ancient Christian work the contest between Christ and Socrates, of which earlier writers had spoken, achieves its true proportions." To delineate the issues involved in that conflict the author contrasts the views presented by Augustine in *The City of God* with those found in Aristophanes' *Assembly of Women*, Plato's *Republic*, Cicero's *Republic*, and the *Apology of Socrates*. It is suggested that Augustine's indictment of each of these works stems from his conviction that they offer an unattainable political ideal.

The essay concludes that for Augustine there is no such thing as a true *res publica* and "no such thing as a Christian polity." The solution Augustine arrived at, in his attempt to synthesize the tenets of Christianity with Greco-Roman philosophy, was to "dispose of the problem of political life, not by integrating the Christian fully into it, but by moving it in the direction of a goal which was not only transpolitical but other-worldly."

22 — _____. **"Augustine's** *City of God* **and the Modern Historical Consciousness."** *Review of Politics* **41 (1979), 323-343.**

In this article the question is asked whether the modern concept of a meaningful and teleological historical movement within a linear temporal scheme has its origin in "Augustine's novel approach to history" as presented in the later books of *De civitate Dei* or departs radically from it. The essay compares the views of Augustine chiefly with those of Eusebius and Orosius on the matter of Christianity, politicism and the nature of empire, and examines the perplexities posed to the human will in the light of divine provi-dence. Through a close look at selected passages from their writ-ings the author observes that what was a solution in the Eusebian and Orosian theories Augustine saw as an "insidious danger" because of the association of Christianity with temporal rewards and the equanimity implied toward both pagans and Christians.

The article concludes that the only similarity between modern and Augustinian concepts of history is "the linear and nonrepeat-able character of the historical process" discussed by Kant and which the author presents as fundamental to the Biblical view of history. Otherwise, an antagonism exists between Christianity and temporal politics and any "notion of a Christian polity . . . is at best a comforting and at worst a fatal illusion."

23 — _____. "The Patristic Sense of Community."
        Augustinian Studies **4 (1973), 179-197.**

This work is a review article of Jeremy D. Adams' book *The Populus of Augustine and Jerome: A Study in the Patristic Sense of Community*. Noting that Adams' methodology finds its closest par-allels in the earlier studies of R. T. Marshall, Gabriel del Estal, Joseph Ratzinger, and Herbert A. Deane, among others, Adams' work is seen as a refinement of the conclusions of his predecessors. "The chief claim to novelty [of this book] lies in its ability to pro-vide a 'set of hard data' on the basis of which it hopefully becomes possible to determine inductively and with great accuracy the full range of meaning that *populus* assumes in Augustine's writings."

The author cites what are regarded as some major weaknesses in Adams' study: 1) an erroneous translation of what Augustine means by "law" and the "role of law in society" in his well-known definition of a people found in Book XIX of *The City of God*; 2) a "pure and simple misreading of Augustine's text" in the discussion of Book X, chapter 13, where Adams suggests that "the Spartans were a people in a fuller sense of the word than the people of God itself"; 3) and a flawed supposition about Augustine's views on the relationship between a *populus* and civil society which "hopelessly blurs the point that Augustine is trying to make." The review con-cludes that "one cannot be sure that the results at which [this study] arrived are entirely reliable in all cases. . . . What we learn from such an exercise is that Augustine's notion of community may be more subtle and complex than is commonly assumed."

See Adams, entry number 1 above.

24 — Frazier, Thomas R. "The Ethics of *The City of God.*" *The Journal of Religious Thought* 26 (1969), 23-36.

Through the combination of a catechetical method of logical inquiry and extensive quotations from *The City of God* this essay seeks to "let Augustine speak for himself." Frazier upholds the image of Augustine as "the great conservative" outlining an ethical philosophy for the Christian *peregrini*. The essay traces the metamorphosis of Augustine's apparent shift from a temporal to an eternal *civitas Dei*. In analyzing this change the article focuses on the subject of ethics with special attention given to the role of love in Augustine's dichotomy; the nature and locus of evil; the end of human endeavor; peace and felicity; virtue; and the balance between passive contemplation and the duty humans have to act responsibly.

25 — Halpern, Richard A. *Spiritual Vision and the* City of God *in* Sir Gawain and the Green Knight. Dissertation. Princeton University, 1976.

The first two chapters of this study identify the central issue of the poem — spiritual vs. carnal vision, life according to the spirit or according to the flesh. Later chapters trace the development of this central conflict in the context of the Augustinian theme of the City of God and the City of Man. The analysis points out that a series of events test Gawain's primary loyalty to God in order that he may learn that "the ability to see spiritual realities behind physical appearances is essential to a right understanding." Gawain's flaw is his "spiritual adultery." He violates his knighthood, breaking faith with his Savior and violating both precepts of the New Law. By means of a list of parallels to Augustine's imagery in *De civitate Dei*, the poem's prologue identifies the history of Britain with Augustine's characterization of the Earthly City, living according to the flesh.

26 — Hartigan, Richard S. "Saint Augustine on War and Killing. The Problem of the Innocent." *Journal of the History of Ideas* **27 (1966), 195-204.**

In the course of this article, the author explicates what he concludes is a "nagging incongruity" between Augustine's private and public ethics contingent upon his distinction between temporal and eternal law. The problem stems from Augustine's "unqualifiedly pacific" views on the matter of Christian private self-defense and his belief that some wars are justifiable. Citing passages in *De civitate Dei* and other works by Augustine, the article supports its argument by examining the issues of authority and obedience, intent, the matters of peace and justice, the goal of the state, and the maintenance of moral order. One particular blind spot in Augustine's argument is his apparent inability to acknowledge the presence of innocent combatants in the army and innocent non-combatants in the society of a just army's enemy. The essay also comments on the bearing of this philosophy on the attitude toward the just war in the Middle Ages.

See Swift, entry number 59 below, for a response to this study.

27 — Hawkins, Peter S. "Polemical Counterpoint in *De Civitate Dei*." *Augustinian Studies* **6 (1975), 97-106.**

Given that the opposition between the *civitas Dei* and the *civitas terrena* is as "fundamental as the strife between truth and falsehood," this essay pursues the role of perception in *The City of God* and discovers that Augustine himself "is obliged to admit a countercurrent of confusion" in the text. The author follows Charles Journet's lead in *L'Englise du verbe Incarne* when he seeks "la presence de la troisieme" somewhere between the two polar cities.

Augustine, in Book V of *The City of God*, reverses the pattern of the first four books when he admits that the pagans had some redeeming qualities. But most astounding in the comparison of the two cities "is the fact that Augustine presents the earthly city not simply as the negative term of a duality, but as an example and standard of what devotion to a community ought to be." The reflection and projection of images becomes crucial to this analysis when Cain, Abel, Romulus, Babylon, Jerusalem, and Rome all become entangled "in a continuum of transformation" which is human history.

While the opposition of the *civitas terrena* and *civitas Dei* remains fundamental, "it is in reality a dialectic, a process not unlike the individual's simultaneous death to the old man and rebirth to the new." The essay concludes that the "compounding and commingling" has not only to do with the fact that both cities experience together all the vicissitudes of the temporal world "as they make their progress (*procursus*) through history. It has to do more radically with a shared nature in the creation of God."

28 — Horton, John T. "The *De Civitate Dei* as Religious Satire." *The Classical Journal* 60 (1964), 193-203.

The claim of this article is that Augustine's use of satire is directly connected to some of the most important themes developed in *De civitate Dei*. In support of this point of view the essay cites a number of passages in which Augustine uses rudeness, ridicule, humor, sarcasm, and even malice in his criticisms of those individuals and ideas that he challenges in his work.

Augustine's use of ridicule is evident in the first chapter of *De civitate Dei* in his attack on the pagans' claim that Christianity caused the fall of Rome. Augustine underscores his ridicule by emphasizing the inadequacy of pagan worship; he suggests that since the deities were unable to protect their own temples, it should not be an occasion for wonder that they were unable to protect the state or the empire. In Augustine's words: "Where then was this crowd of deities when, long before the ancient manners were corrupted, Rome was taken and burnt by the Gauls? If the gods were present, were they perchance asleep?"

Augustine's rhetorical use of rudeness and sarcasm is seen in his severe condemnation of Rome when he proposes that the Romans "had been so impiously unjust that they did not deserve even to be called a people." Citing Cicero as his authority, Augustine turns the Roman's definition of justice against them and charges them with injustice. According to Augustine, for the Romans, "justice is that virtue which distributes to each his own." Augustine asks: "What therefore is the justice of man which takes man himself away from the true God and subjects him to unclean evils? Is this to distribute to each his own?"

Finally, Augustine's satiric use of humor is evident in the pleasure he takes in suggesting that geese might have been better guardians than the gods in defending the city against the Gauls. The distribution of powers among the Roman deities is made to seem especially ridiculous. "We laugh indeed," says Augustine, "when we see the gods assigned through human invention to a mutual division of labor, as if they were little farmers of the revenue or workers in the silversmiths' quarter." In Augustine's view, this division of labor does not "comport with divine dignity." Other aspects of the arrangement of things in the pagan pantheon of gods and goddesses are also mentioned in this essay as evidence of Augustine's use of wry humor in his challenge to the ideas of his adversaries. The author concludes by noting that "Augustine, like any first-rate satirist, makes his satire all the more pungent by giving it a sober purpose."

29 — Johnson, Penelope D. *"Virtus*: Transition from Classical Latin to the *De Civitate Dei." Augustinian Studies* 6 (1975), 117-124.

The meanings of *virtus*, from old Latin and through the writings of Cicero and Sallust to Augustine, is the subject of this article which examines the implications of the word in matters political and theological. Johnson sees its original meaning of "magic or miraculous power" transformed into civic virtue with the growth of the Roman republic and empire only to regain its miraculous connotation, while still highly politicized, in *De civitate Dei*. In *The City of God virtus* is a divine gift from God. "As Augustinian *virtus* had both a divine origin and a divine goal, 'miraculous power' was again functioning in it. . . . Whatever the conscious intention, *virtus* in *De civitate Dei* echoed its earliest meaning, and gave to the Christian vocabulary of the Middle Ages, *virtus* as *ordo amoris*."

The three authors discussed in the essay are seen as using *virtus* in ways that parallel their own relationships to the rise and fall of Rome and the role of the individual in the temporal state. The article also briefly examines Augustine's concept of *virtus* as it figures in his refutation of Pelagius.

30 — Kilzer, Ernest. "The Social Thought of St. Augustine." *The American Benedictine Review* **3 (1962), 293-335.**

This essay serves as a general introduction to Augustine's theological view of history and society by summary of the major doctrinal issues developed in *The City of God*: the idea of the two cities, time and history, society and the state, slavery, property, work and occupations, the church, and the Augustinian concept of law. The author concludes that despite "the Aristotelian revolution" of the thirteenth century, the social thought of St. Augustine remained a major source of inspiration for later periods, "mainly because it was an explicit and powerful expression of Christian teachings."

31 — Korfmacher, William C. "Four Notes on the *De Civitate Dei*.**"** *Classical Folia* **14 (1960), 82-85.**

As the title indicates, this essay consists of four brief notes on the *De civitate Dei*. In the first note, "State to Man and Man to State," the author observes that whereas Plato in the *Republic* proceeds from "justice in the state to justice in the individual man" Augustine in *De civitate Dei* (Book IV, ch. 4) proceeds in "just the opposite way — moving from individual men to states." The second note, "Beneficence of the 'Sense-line Approach,' " comments on Augustine's sentence construction. The author suggests that while many of the sentences of the *De civitate Dei* are rhetorically effective, they are exceedingly difficult because of their length and involvement. The author proposes that the "so-called 'sense-line method' which depends ultimately on the ancient arrangement of prose *per cola et commata*" is extremely helpful in arriving at a full understanding of the text.

The third section, "Word and Fact," refers to the contrast the Greeks and Romans drew among the terms, "word," "fact," and "deed," and it remarks on the use Augustine makes of these distinctions in his tribute in Book Six (ch. 2) to the learning of Varro. And, finally, in the fourth note, "Janus and 'Gaining Face,' " the author cites Augustine's reference to "gaining face" in the seventh book (ch. 4) of the *De civitate Dei* and suggests that in Augustine's view just as "'losing face' is to one's discredit, 'gaining face' is in one's favor."

32 — LaCroix, Richard R. "Augustine on the Simplicity of God."
   New Scholasticism **51 (1977), 453-469.**

This essay develops a comprehensive critique of the logic behind Augustine's doctrine of divine simplicity. The author joins those philosophers who are "puzzled" by Augustine's claim that "God is absolutely distinguishable from every other thing by virtue of the fact that He alone is simple while every other nature is without exception manifold."

The article begins its analysis of Augustine's concept of divine simplicity with the detailed account of the doctrine given by Augustine in *The City of God*, XI, 10. Augustine says: "a nature is said to be simple on the grounds that it cannot lose any of the properties that it possesses; that is, there is no distinction to be made between what that nature is and the properties that it has." The author's argument focuses on the issues of contingent vs. necessary properties of being, the distinction between relative and nonrelative contingent properties, the relationship of properties to a being's nature, and the matters of God's omniscience and the stability of his properties.

After attempting to draw each of Augustine's propositions to its logical end by means of its manifold logical and philosophical implications, the essay concludes that Augustine's distinction between essential properties of being, his account of the concept of unchangeableness, and his account of simplicity itself are all incoherent within the framework of his own explication in *The City of God* and *De Trinitate*, V, 8.

33 — Laoye, John A. *Augustine's Apologetic Use of the Old Testament*
   as Reflected Especially in the **De Civitate Dei. Dissertation.**
   Southern Baptist Theology Seminary, 1972.

This study examines the way in which Augustine used the Old Testament in his refutation of pagan accusations and in his vindication of the truth of the Christian faith. The first chapter reviews the life of Augustine, his age, his church and the major intellectual movements that had significant impact on his thought. Chapter two examines the view of the origin and validity of the authority of

the Scriptures in the early church. Chapter three discusses the role
of the Old Testament in Christian apologetics before Augustine. It
is argued that Augustine "inherited the allegorical method of exegesis from the earlier Christian apologists and that he adapted and
perfected it in his defense of the Christian faith."

Chapter four shows how Augustine appealed to the Old Testament Law and Prophets in his attempts to establish the authenticity
of Christianity. And chapter five focuses on Augustine's apologetic
use of the Old Testament in *De civitate Dei*. The writer concludes
that Augustine "saw the culmination of the history of the two cities
in heaven and hell as the fulfillment of the Old Testament predic-
tions."

34 — Lavere, George J. "Metaphor and Symbol in St. Augustine's
***De Civitate Dei*." In *Collectanea Augustiniana*. Ed. Joseph**
C. Schnaubelt and Frederick VanFleteren. New York:
Peter Lang, 1990. Pp. 225-243.

This study offers a detailed discussion of the major symbols and
metaphors used by Augustine in *De civitate Dei*. The key to an
understanding of Augustine's interpretation of human history is
found in his metaphorical use of the two cities — one city of the
flesh and the other of the spirit. The author notes that "the root of
the metaphor lies in the indisputably evident fact of human attrac-
tion to and love of certain objects." The literary status of the *De
civitate Dei* thus "pivots upon the symbolic and metaphorical use of
this notion of 'two cities.' " Augustine makes extensive use of the
symbolic function of Scripture to explicate his text. The true
importance of Scripture "is not in its biblical context . . . rather it is
the symbolic and prophetic significance of the details it offers in
relation to the reality of the city of God." For Augustine, it is
through an allegorical interpretation of Scripture that its fundamental meaning emerges. Similarly, the key to an accurate interpretation of the *De civitate Dei* rests upon a genuine understanding
of the metaphorical and symbolic structure Augustine uses in
developing the major themes which run throughout the work.

35 —_____. "Camus' *Plague* and Saint Augustine's *Civitas Terrena*." *Proceedings of the PMR Conference* 10 (1985), 87-98.

This article offers an Augustinian reading of Camus' *Plague*, citing the similarities between the *civitas terrena* of *De civitate Dei* and Camus' Oran. It is noted that the *civitas terrena* and Oran are representative of the human race as two societies with no clear lines of spiritual and moral demarcation. Both Augustine and Camus consider questions of theodicy and take a pessimistic view toward earthly existence. And "both employ the notion of city as a point of departure in the elaboration of a metaphor extending to the whole of humanity."

According to the author, the plague serves as an apocalyptic crisis which serves to distinguish good citizens from evil citizens. Some individuals work against the plague risking life-threatening exposure to the disease. Others are content to profit from the misery of their fellow citizens. The article concludes that in *The Plague*, as in *The City of God*, "humanity is divided by the choices its members make, by what they love and their success or failure in life is measured by the degree to which they achieve the object of their desires." Like Augustine, for Camus also humankind divides into those who love God and those who love themselves, either as individuals or collectively as humanity. In Oran, as in Rome, the inhabitants are at once united, since all are citizens of the earthly city, and divided, based upon their "love of God" or their "love of self."

36 —_____. "The Influence of Saint Augustine on Early Medieval Political Theory." *Augustinian Studies* 12 (1981), 1-9.

The Augustinian distinction between the City of God and the City of Man, their commingling in the *civitas terrena*, and the disputation of authority arising from this interrelationship in the organization of the medieval church and its role in the state are examined in the cases of three important early medieval political theorists — Gelasius I, Gregory the Great, and Isidore of Seville. Beginning with Augustine's reluctant concession that the state is a necessary alternative to anarchy in the *civitas terrena*, the essay traces the evolution of the papacy-monarchy struggle and some of its politico-theological controversies from the fifth to the seventh centuries.

Citing *De civitate Dei* V and Augustine's position in the Donatist controversy, it is argued that Augustine establishes a philosophy for Christian kingship which proposes that the state is "the morally neutral agency of coercive power which holds the earthly city together while its inhabitants make the ultimate personal choice of God or self." Augustine was a "political realist" who drew a careful distinction between secular authority and papal authority. The neo-Augustinian political theorists, on the other hand, tended to draw the state into the Church, "even to the point of absorbing the functions of the state by the Church."

37 — _____. "The Political Realism of Saint Augustine."
      Augustinian Studies **11 (1980), 135-144.**

The composition of *The City of God* as a defense of Christianity against the very real political criticism levied at it is the starting point of this essay. Augustine's practical points in the response to the charges that Rome fell because Christianity subverted the empire are outlined as evidence for his earthly political astuteness. Nevertheless, "Augustine's reply . . . moves far beyond the particular circumstances of Rome." The key to understanding Augustine's "political realism" is "the chronic condition of civil war" which has always plagued humankind.

Augustine's view of the political state, it is contended, is that it is a necessary evil. Contrary to his predecessor Origen — who saw the dominion of the Roman empire as divinely ordained to facilitate the teachings of Christ — and Hippolytus — who saw it as "the apocalyptic beast described in the *Book of Daniel*" — Augustine considered the state an "unpredictable admixture on all levels of the functioning *civitas terrena*." By its nature the temporal state seeks to rule by domination, and because it fails to execute perfect divine justice it is the agent of injustice. But, paradoxically, "despite all appearances to the contrary, its goal is peace," and by dispensing its crude form of justice it encourages humankind toward the good "by means of its restrictive and punitive measures."

38 — _____. **"The Problem of the Common Good in Saint Augustine's** *Civitas Terrena.*" *Augustinian Studies* **14 (1983), 1-10.**

This essay begins by asking: "If the earthly city—the *civitas terrena*—enclosed within its boundaries the two mystical cities, the City of God and the City of Man, each with its own good and its own attachment to its respective good, how, on these terms, could there be an earthly city in any proper sense of the definition of political association? What would be the common good of the body politic as a whole?" The author reviews Augustine's expansion in Book II, Chapter 21 of *The City of God* of the Ciceronian criticism of the Roman state and then proceeds to analyze the question of the common good in light of the contemporary schism within Roman society.

The essay compares Cicero's and Augustine's views on the meaning of justice and the relationship between true justice and a genuine commonwealth. The source of conflict in Augustine's political philosophy rises from the fact that he "offers two definitions of a 'people' and, consequently, two definitions of the state. . .

[There is] the actual existence within the *civitas terrena* of two distinct societies, each with its own conception of the common good and the meaning of justice." The author sees Augustine's political views—"his political realism"—as grounded in "his realization of the inability of the earthly city to accomplish its task of mediation."

39 — MacKinnon, Patricia L. *The Analogy of the Body Politic in St. Augustine, Dante, Petrarch, and Ariosto.* **Dissertation. University of California, 1988.**

Chapter one of this work, "St. Augustine's *De Civitate Dei*: The Divided Self/The Divided *Civitas*," traces the governing analogy between the individual and the body politic, borrowed from Plato's *Republic*, in *The City of God*. The author argues that the Platonic analogy between the self and the *civitas* is exploited by Augustine as the key figure in his analysis of the doomed nature of the *civitas terrena*, and that it underlies the relation he perceives between fragmentation in the soul and the political fragmentation of civil and foreign wars. According to this study, what most distinguishes *The City of God* from other Augustinian texts is the extent to which it is based not merely upon the Platonic heritage but rather on one particular Platonic text, the *Republic*.

The link between the governing idea of the *Republic* and the conceptual framework of *The City of God* is found in Augustine's definition of the "two cities." His notion of two communities — *civitas terrena* and *civitas Dei* — builds upon Plato's "fundamental axiom that the relations internal to the individual soul are the index and determining factor of the form of polity." The notion of two contrasting cities competing for the individual's earthly allegiance is also found in Plato's speculation about human destiny in this life and the destination of the soul beyond historical time. And Plato's one "right" city becomes Augustine's unique *civitas Dei*. Lastly, as the author puts it, "Plato's claim that the inner rectitude of the soul is its own reward and may be judged by the happiness or unhappiness of its possessor, acquires an eschatological emphasis in Augustine upon ultimate spiritual polarities — the felicity of eternal life as opposed to the misery of damnation."

40 — MacQueen, D. J. "The Origin and Dynamics of Society and the State According to St. Augustine." *Augustinian Studies* **4 (1973), 73-101.**

As the author puts it, this article deals with Augustine's doctrine of the state, its origins and its structure. For Augustine the state has its origins in the concept of society; and, since it is a product of the order of the universe, society, or the state, is thus itself hierarchically structured — i.e., it consists of a series of units arranged in ascending order.

The essay analyzes Augustine's views on the idea of *ordo rerum* (universal order) and the concept of *bonum commune* (common good). Having inherited these notions from the Graeco-Roman tradition, Augustine adapts them to what the author describes as "distinctively Christian insights." For Augustine, "God is not merely the Summit of order; . . . [order] actually originates within the Godhead itself." In Augustine's notion of *bonum commune*, "charity has replaced, or at any rate, transcended the classical virtues of *humanitas* and *magnitudo*." And in Augustinian thought the "only true ultimate Common Good" is God himself.

The study discusses Augustine's views on the origins of the *civitas terrena* and the *civitas Dei* and traces the relationship between Augustine's *civitas terrena* and earlier definitions of and criteria for membership in a *res publica*. Such terms as society, state, commonwealth, community, fellowship, and citizenship are analyzed with respect to their similarities and differences. The author argues that Augustine, by adding the word *Dei* (of God) to *civitas*, in effect "applies a criterion or selective principle that isolates for consideration one distinctive *civitas* from the many which have existed in the past and will appear in the future." According to the essay, the term which most nearly conveys what Augustine means by *societas* is "fellowship."

The article includes a discussion of Augustine's critique of the Ciceronian doctrine of justice. Augustine abandoned the idea that justice is the unifying bond of a state and produced in its place a new concept of the state based on a *differentia* other than justice. Augustine proposes that love is the true social bond of a society. In the author's words: "Rejecting justice as the bond of union, he therefore proposes an entirely different and original definition of a people: an association of rational beings united by the agreement of all its members upon a common object of love."

Other aspects of Augustinian thought that are dealt with in the essay include the influence of the Stoic notion of society upon Augustine and of the Graeco-Roman attitude to the institution of friendship. It is pointed out that despite their many similarities, Augustine's doctrine significantly departs from accepted classical thought in corresponding areas. Also discussed are Augustine's concept of a "hierarchy of ordained loves," the notions of pride and humility, the two kinds of love which founded two mystical societies and, finally, the relationship between love and order in society, on the one hand, and between order and disorder in universal society on the other.

41 — Markus, Robert A. "*De Civitate Dei*: Pride and the Common Good." *Proceedings of the PMR Conference* **12-13 (1987-88), 1-16. Rpt. in** *Collectanea Augustiniana.* **Ed. Joseph C. Schnaubelt, O.S.A. and Frederick Van Fleteren. New York: Peter Lang, 1990. Pp. 245-259.**

This essay deals with the theme of the common good in the *De civitate Dei*. Acknowledging that the idea of the common good is not central to the work, it nonetheless "lurks in the background . . . and is there from the start." Since Augustine's purpose in *De civitate Dei* was to develop a notion of civil community which would make it possible for Christians to participate in its activities, the concept of pride would necessarily play an important role.

The author points out that Augustine, in his early works, holds a fairly traditional attitude toward pride: first, it is conceived in terms of the mind "going outside itself" and attaching to "material things," and second, it is viewed as a "breach of the rational order." In brief, Augustine's view of pride is "that it is the root of sin, and that sin is the breach of order." The study notes, however, that there are subtle and important changes in the way Augustine later discusses the theme of pride. By the time he came to write Book XIX of *De civitate Dei*, the concept of pride was central to his discussion of the relation between the "two cities" and actual societies. At the center of Augustine's mature view of pride there is a duality: "government seen as domination and government seen as guardian of the common good." From this viewpoint, in a politically organized society pride is ameliorated when it is used correctly, that is, when it is used on behalf of the common good.

42 — McKee, Donald K. "Augustine's Political Thought." *The Drew Gateway* **40 (1970), 80-87.**

Following a summary of Augustine's political theory, the author reviews Augustine's criteria for membership in either the *civitas terrena* or the *civitas Dei* and proposes that no individual enjoys exclusive membership in either city but, rather, that "everyone, every single person, belongs to both realms." Augustine's political philosophy is permeated by both idealism and realism. On the one hand, "the Godly City furnishes moral direction for human striving, something of a goal for social and political activity." Yet, human nature "makes the City of God ultimately transcendent. The ethical perfection of this realm can never be attained in history because self-love and self-interest are permanent aspects of the human situation."

The article identifies three basic Augustinian principles which the author argues are "logically disharmonious." First, the salvation doctrine which separates those elect of the City of God from the remainder in the worldly city. Second, the ethical definition of the two cities which states that the sojourning City of God in the earthly realm is a community without manifestations of self-love while the earthly city is a sphere of self-interest only. And third, the view of human nature which proposes "that redeemed men remain sinners but no person is totally depraved."

The author explores three possible logical solutions by which these ambiguities in Augustine's thought might be resolved but concludes that each solution alters crucial elements of Augustinian doctrine and theory which "Augustine himself would not countenance."

43 — McKinley, Mary B. *"The City of God* and the City of Man: Limits of Language in Montaigne's 'Apologie.'" *Romanic Review* **71 (1980), 122-140.**

The author begins by mentioning that several scholars, starting with Villey, have noted that *The City of God* is "a vital presence in [Montaigne's] *Essais.*" This study, on the other hand, examines the considerable influence *The City of God* exerted on Montaigne's "Apologie." Augustine's dichotomy between the two cities and his observations on "the very possibility of articulating the notion of God" initiate Montaigne's own treatment of the inadequacies of language. The author compares the similar views which the two men held on the matters of discourse and anthropomorphism in addition to the role of digressions in discourse. The differences between them are also discussed.

The City of God "is predicated upon a clearly preconceived eschatological scheme" from which nothing ultimately deters it. Montaigne, however, exhibits an obvious preference for the detours and thereby directs his linguistic pilgrimage toward the city of man rather than the city of God, "renouncing the Augustinian aspiration to the divine realm of silence." In brief, the main focus is not on Montaigne's departure from Augustinian theology but on Montaigne's divergence from Augustine in matters of "poetics and the way a writer views the medium of his creation: language."

44 — Martin, Rex. "The Two Cities in Augustine's Political Philosophy." *Journal of the History of Ideas* **33 (1972), 195-216.**

This study seeks to produce "a single, coherent reading" of the Augustinian concept of the state by examining three crucial themes and passages: the notion of the two cities and the political interpretation associated with it; the analogy drawn in *The City of God* IV.4 between a kingdom (*regnum*) and a robber band; and Augustine's analysis and reformulation of Cicero's definition of a commonwealth (*res publica*). The author challenges the "identification model" which links the Earthly City with the state and the City of God with the institutional church, and substitutes for it the idea of "agent representation" — "there are earthly institutions that 'represent' and do the work of the two cities in human history: the imperial states are special embodiments of the City of Earth and, after the advent of Christ, the institutional church is the unique and indispensable representative of the City of God."

To support this assertion the essay examines the modifications which Augustine made to the Ciceronian idea of a *res publica*. In sum, the more "feasible" definition Augustine promised in II.21 is a devaluation of the idealized classical state which operates under a strict code of justice in favor of a "'well-ordered concord' in which obedience follows from a rational conception of permanent and mutual interests and not from fear and repression." The City of Earth does not refer to the state per se but, rather, to the "love of ruling" which Augustine associates with the imposed rule of an "imperial state." What Augustine actually favors is a commonwealth founded upon "common agreement." And for Augustine the foundation of a true *res publica* is the "tranquillity of order" which results from this common agreement.

45 — Nikkel, David H.   "St. Augustine on the Goodness of Creaturely Existence." *Duke Divinity Review* **43 (1978), 181-187.**

Two apparently disparate passages in *The City of God* XXII are the focus of this essay (i.e., XXII,22 and XXII,24). The former is a litany of worldly miseries, the latter a list of worldly joys. The author seeks not to reconcile the antitheses but to show how they are indicative of Augustine's struggle between affirming and denying temporal and earthly things. The essay proposes that the antitheses form an integral part of a process of affirming "spatiotemporal goods as gifts from God." The essay argues that in his later years, particularly in *The City of God*, Augustine "exhibits a greater affirmation than heretofore of human existence in an environment in time."

46 — Nugent, Donald. *"The City of God* **Revisited."** *Cross Currents* **19 (1969), 241-255.**

Augustine's analysis of the cultural dialectic between the cities of God and Man informs and guides this essay. The author gives a sweeping summary of Western politico-theological history from the fall of Rome to the post-modern era in an attempt to see the resurgence of spirituality in the late nineteen sixties as part of a larger historical movement. The metaphysical orientation of the hippie culture and the avant-garde status of *homo religiosus* serve as springboards for the author's evaluation. The essay is a "reflection and a variation of an old theme, extending Augustine, as it were, forward in time. . . . The underlying assumption has been that man is naturally a religious as well as a political animal, and that these categories must be at once related and distinct."

47 — O'Donnell, James J.   "The Inspiration for Augustine's *De Civitate Dei."* *Augustinian Studies* **10 (1979), 75-79.**

Given that Augustine's idea of the two cities substantially predates the *De civitate Dei* and also that the concept was initially an anti-heretical polemic, the author asks, "why develop an anti-heretical idea at length in a treatise ostensibly directed against paganism?" In the author's view the expansion of the two cities idea into *De civitate Dei* was a "stroke of genius" when we consider the historical circumstances under which it was written.

In Augustine's day the metaphor of *peregrini* (strangers) exiled from their true *patria* (home) carried a universal significance. The fall of Rome resulted in the exodus of Romans of all religious persuasions — Christian and pagan — from Italy into North Africa. The essay argues that the situation of the refugees was "analogous, in legal terms, to the kind of behavior which [Augustine] wanted to preach as most suitable for Christians living in the earthly city." The refugees came to North Africa not as permanent citizens but as strangers. They were citizens of Rome, a distant city, and only *peregrini* in North Africa. They lamented their exile from their great city and they looked forward to the day when they could return to their true *patria*.

In a concluding comment the essay mentions that Augustine's "redirection in [*De civitate Dei*] of the notion of two cities left itself open to one almost inevitable misinterpretation, . . . a misinterpretation which was in fact made by Orosius" and which was the cause of "a kind of Christian imperalism" in the Middle Ages.

48 — _____. *Augustine*. Boston: G. K. Hall, 1985.

This book is a general introduction to Augustine and his ideas. Chapter 3, "Christianity and Society," is devoted to *The City of God*. The essay places *The City of God* within the historical circumstances in which it was written; it discusses Augustine's purpose in writing the work; and it presents an overview of the thematic structure of the twenty-two books which comprise the work. The main focus is on a discussion of Augustine's views on the nature of reality from the perspective of Christianity. This theme is explored by reviewing Augustine's ideas about the "world of appearances" and the "world of reality" and, in turn, by examining his views on the relationship between Christianity and society. Augustine's purpose in writing *The City of God* was to discuss how "Christianity proposed that men and women go about living in the real, fallen world."

49 — O'Donovan, Oliver. **"Augustine's** *City of God* **XIX and Western Political Thought."** *Dionysius* **11 (1987), 89-110.**

The purpose of this essay is to demonstrate that *The City of God* is a study in social and political philosophy. In this context, the author concentrates on two features of Augustine's text. First, the way in which the work "anticipates modern Western political thought, in its separation between society and virtue." And second, the way the work appears "alien to modernity in its failure to allow for the progressive transformation of the social order."

According to the author, Augustine, in his new definition of the true meaning of justice, introduced the first standard of modern political thought by "casting the political community off from its moorings in justice." This departure from classical theory results from the change Augustine makes to Cicero's definition of justice, namely, "the removal of the reference to right." Augustine breaks the link between society and virtue and substitutes in its place a view which gives "due recognition both to the reality of the moral order which makes social existence possible and to its fundamentally flawed character." The essay concludes that Augustine does not disparage the role of virtue in political life but, rather, that he demonstrates "an ability to discern shadows cast by virtue in surprising places."

Augustine's political thought is least modern in perspective in that it lacks a theory of progress. In Augustinian thought human history is "a demonic history, which expresses the divine purpose only as providence, following its own hidden course, uses it to higher ends." For Augustine, "the final good is social, not political, and that final good cannot be realized in this life."

50 — Ojeman, Mary R. *Sancti Augustini* De Civitate Dei *Liber Primus: A Sense-Line Arrangement, English Translation, and Rhetorical Study.* **Dissertation. Saint Louis University, 1960.**

This study of the first book of *De civitate Dei* offers a sense-line analysis of the Latin text, "the purpose of which for the modern reader is that it presents the sentences in unified wholes, embraced in almost a single eye-span, with each member fitting into its proper relationship to the other members." Syntax, rhythm, and emotion are determinative factors in this arrangement of the sense-line, though quite often "the only criterion for marking off a passage is that it makes sense." The text used is the edition of Bernardus Dombart and Alphonsis Kalb.

The most frequently found figures are those of parallelism, but other evidences of Augustine's skill are also mentioned. The study notes that Saint Augustine's purpose is to move and instruct, rather than lavishly to display his rhetorical arts. A glossary of terms defining the figures as they are used in this study is provided, and a table citing the frequency of use of the various figures is also included.

51 — O'Meara, John. *Charter of Christendom: The Significance of The City of God*. New York: Macmillan, 1961.

The first part of this work places *The City of God* in its historical situation, traces, in earlier writings of Augustine, formulations of what became the main theme of the work, and describes, using Augustine's own words, its contents and order. The second part, which is in three divisions, considers *The City of God* from three angles: its interpretation of the Bible, its attitude to Greek philosophy, and its attitude to Rome.

The first section, "The Bible," argues that Augustine's final authority for the points made in *The City of God* is the scriptures. As the author puts it: "The whole approach of the book is from the viewpoint of the Scriptures, and the matter of the larger second part is, in addition, taken from the Bible." Augustine's confidence in the Bible is seen in the many passages where he talks about the fulfillment of its prophecies and the miracles of Christianity. It is also revealed in the fact that a large number of his writings are scriptural commentaries, and, finally, that the last twelve books of *The City of God* are, as the author puts it, "the exposition of certain fundamental teachings of Revelation."

The second section, "Greek Philosophy," challenges the view put forth by many scholars that Augustine's thought was dominated by Platonism or Neoplatonism. It is argued that while Augustine indicates many points of agreement between Christianity and the Platonists, it nonetheless remains that Augustine's true position is that "Christianity comes first, Platonism second." In spite of their many similarities, Platonism has tenets which radically depart from Christian doctrine and which Augustine seriously attacks throughout *The City of God*, particularly in his discussion of the philosophy of Porphyry. Acknowledging that Augustine was persuaded, at the time of his conversion, that Platonism provided a rational explanation of many things, his enthusiasm for it had nonetheless declined considerably by the time he was composing *The City of God*.

The third section, "Rome," deals with the idea that there is nothing in *The City of God* itself to support the proposition that the work offers "a theory of an ideal State." Even though Rome is the background for the context of the work, Augustine's ultimate attitude toward the Roman Empire is that it "was *absolutely* evil; but *relatively* had a limited goodness." Rome lacked true justice and therefore could not be a true *res publica* but, since its other "natural virtues are an ideal base on which religion builds the citizen of the City of God," it thus had a special purpose in God's divine plan. In sum, for Augustine the state is an instrument in human salvation.

52 — Raitiere, Martin N. "More's *Utopia* and *The City of God*."
***Studies in the Renaissance* 20 (1973), 144-168.**

This article compares Augustine's *The City of God* and More's *Utopia* to show that More's work embodies many of the same views as Augustine's. The essay discusses Augustine's and More's ideas on various subjects including the idea of community, the function of the state, natural law, patriarchalism, the concept of justice, the notion of *dominium*, Christian versus civic obligation, and the doctrine of the just war.

The essay points out that scholars generally do not find any substantial evidence of a direct influence of Augustine's classic on More's work. The author argues, however, that conjecture about Augustinian influence on Utopia is justified within the context of the "metaphysical dimension" of the two works. From this perspective, *The City of God* is seen "as a possible source not of specific social doctrines but rather of More's *facetudo* vis-a-vis the realm of politics." The study concludes that the similarities between Augustine's work and More's result, finally, from the concern in both works with the relationship between the Christian imperatives and those of the *vita socialis*. It is the discontinuity between politics and Christian obligation that Augustine in *The City of God* and More in the *Utopia* wanted to illuminate.

53 — Reis, Linda M. The City of God: *St. Augustine's Christian Philosophy of History.* **Master of Divinity Thesis. Phillips University, 1987.**

This thesis is an analysis of Augustine's *The City of God* as Augustine's theology or philosophy of history. The present study does not distinguish between the two terms because Augustine, in his usage of the terms, "makes no such distinction."

Chapter I, the introduction, consists of a general discussion of Augustine's view of all reality in order that we may better understand what the City of God means to him. Chapter II deals with Augustine's doctrine of creation and God's administration of the created order. Chapter III presents an investigation into Augustine's concept of time, as it is presented in the *Confessions* and in *The City of God*. Chapter IV discusses Augustine's break with the cyclic theory of history and his development of the concept of history as the story of two cities. Chapter V describes Augustine's eschatology and vision of God.

This work offers an eschatological investigation of Augustine's Christian view of history. The emphasis of the study, as the author points out, is on "the end of time which sees humanity as being in process toward a not yet attained but ultimate condition of humankind." From this perspective, human history is seen to be a continuing and increasing fulfillment of the redemption.

54 — Reuther, Rosemary Radford. "Augustine and Christian Political Theology." *Interpretation* **29 (1975), 252-265.**

The relation of the "political dimension of theology" to the "*status quo*" of either secular or ecclesiastical establishments is the subject of this essay. The author begins by reviewing the history of this tension within the Judaic tradition and the ferment it proved to be for the emergence of Christianity. The extreme duality of Jewish apocalypticism was a formative influence upon the early Christian church which was itself largely politically apostatic.

Nevertheless, internal debate persisted on the responsibility and destiny of the church as a political entity until Augustine sought "to combine them into a new synthesis" in *The City of God*. Noting that Augustine was a man steeped in both politico-religious extremes the author sees him as confirming the imperial *status quo* of Roman Catholicism as well as its ostensible antithesis, "the empire . . . as a strictly secular realm organized for legitimate secular purposes." Thus Augustine is credited with first recognizing in theological history an autonomously valid secular political order. The essay proposes, however, that in so far as *The City of God* presents temporal existence as inconsequential, Augustine "fails to answer the question of the ultimate meaning of the human, historical project itself."

55 — Smalley, Beryl. *English Friars and Antiquity in the Early Fourteenth Century.* **New York: Barnes & Noble, 1960.**

This study includes a discussion of the writings of two early fourteenth-century English friars who wrote on Augustine's *De civitate Dei*. The commentaries by Thomas Waleys and John Ridevall are viewed by the author as pieces of "solid scholarship" which make a significant contribution to the study of Augustine's most widely-known work. It is also noted that because the friars wrote for a lay audience, their commentaries "played a significant role in popularizing a knowledge and understanding of Augustine's *De civitate Dei*."

Thomas Waleys' "Commentary on *De civitate Dei*, I-X," published in 1332, focuses on an examination of the many allusions that Augustine uses in the first ten books of *The City of God*. Waleys limits his task to the first ten books because, in view of their numerous references to histories and fables, they seemed to him to need special explanation. Waleys shows that earlier scholarship on *The City of God* was not only partial in its scope but that it often seriously erred in its conclusions. The main interest of Waleys' study is to demonstrate the inadequacy of Trevet's earlier commentary on Augustine's work. The essay claims that Waleys' intention was to "improve on his senior." That he succeeded in his purpose is seen in the fact that his commentary, according to the essay, "became a classic."

Like Waleys, John Ridevall found Trevet's commentary insufficient and began by writing his own essay as a critique of the older scholar's work. His "Commentary on *De civitate Dei*," however, developed into a detailed analysis of the pagan deities referred to in *The City of God*. Ridevall's method is to create a scheme which makes it possible for him to describe the pantheon and to organize a catalog of the ancient gods and goddesses on the basis of their "greatness." It is noted that Ridevall's approach was to divide pagan deities into twenty-two classes, "each corresponding to a book of *De civitate Dei*," and proceed to show how each of the twenty-two books attacks "the cult of a special sort of god or goddess."

The author concludes that of the two friars Ridevall is the better interpreter of Augustine. Ridevall's strong Christian bent resulted in his interest in the *mens Augustini*. In contrast, for Waleys, Augustine was merely a "gateway to antiquity."

56 — Smith, Sharon Off Dunlap. *Illustrations of Raoul de Praelles' Translation of St. Augustine's* **City of God** *Between 1375 and 1420*. **Dissertation. New York University, 1974.**

This work concerns itself with the cycle of illustrations, one for each of the twenty-two books, accompanying the presentation copy to Charles V of Raoul de Praelles' French translation of *The City of God*. This was the first time that a full cycle of illustrations was produced. The study examines "several families of manuscripts to determine the degree to which the origin of other cycles and the workshops in which they were produced can be correlated."

The following method of investigation is used: each workshop is studied, the dates of the manuscripts are reviewed, and the iconography of the miniatures is analyzed. The author also attempts to establish who was responsible for the program of illumination — the *chef d'atelier* or a scholarly intermediary. The study determines the dates of the manuscripts, settles questions of iconography, and establishes the identity of the workshops. And it concludes that "the scholar, Jacques Courau, initiated the cycle of miniatures for the Master's model."

57 — Snyder, David C. "Augustine's Concept of Justice and Civil Government." *Christian Scholar's Review* **14 (1985), 244-256.**

The City of God is here seen as a doctrinal work which is "not systematic but polemical." Thus the author seeks to extract the political from out of the apologetic "by first describing the key Augustinian notions of justice and the nature and purpose of civil government, and then arguing that despite his efforts to think biblically, the great African bishop gives us an unacceptable view."

First considered is the fundamental antithesis between the *civitas terrena* and the *civitas Dei*. According to the two loves on which the two cities are founded, Snyder illustrates that the evil and good comprising each of the cities is not part and parcel of the cities per se but dependent upon the individual members of those cities. From this he concludes that justice also depends upon the just qualities of the individual person. He agrees with other Augustine scholars that it is incorrect to identify either city with the earthly church and state and shows how the discussion in *The City of God* of the Ciceronian republic is used by Augustine to demonstrate that the state is imperfect, unnatural, and remedial.

Snyder finds logical inconsistencies in Augustine's view of the civil state as a necessary evil and dispenser of injustice because Augustine's logic, he contends, does not maintain the initial antithesis of his cosmos. The proportionate population of just and unjust men in either city does not reflect the quality of justice in each; therefore, Augustine's condemnation of the state is unwarranted "because justice cannot be the defining characteristic of a state." What unites any state is the unqualified "common love" of its members. A further inconsistency in Augustine's thought, it is argued, is that in accepting the remedial role of the state, he admits its acquisition of goodness by its imitation, however slight, of divine perfection. Thus "the state can practice a modicum of justice because traces of God's justice remain in all individuals."

Finally, the author presents "two mistakes" made by Augustine on justice and government. He is in error in supposing that the state is "unnatural, originating in sin" because there are many necessary functions of government that even a sinless society would require. And secondly, the individualistic concept of justice is unfounded because just people are capable of instituting unjust policies. And, injustices can result from a combination of factors over which persons have no control.

58 — Swift, Louis J. "Defining *Gloria* **in Augustine's** *City of God.***"
In** *Diakonia: Studies in Honor of Robert T. Meyer.* **Ed.
Thomas Halton and Joseph P. Williman. Washington:
Catholic University of America Press, 1986.**

The intention of this essay is to demonstrate that when Augustine deals with the theme of *gloria* in *The City of God*, he uses the term in three different senses. First, *gloria* is linked with *libido dominandi* and with moral decline in the life of the Roman state. Second, Augustine defines *gloria Christiana* in a way that "reflects both a continuity with traditional Roman concepts and a sharp departure from them." In sum, whereas the Roman citizen found fulfillment in the recognition achieved in this lifetime, *gloria* is for Christians a reality outside time. Finally, in his text Augustine offers a brief delineation of *cupiditas gloriae*, the glory that is stimulated by a passion for renown.

Since in historical terms divine providence works through human actions, those individuals who resist the vice of avarice and who pursue glory for noble aims are, in fact, placing limits on their own *amor sui*. And it is this which distinguishes them from those who are subject to the *libido dominandi* and from the Christian faithful. As the author notes, "from this perspective, then, it seems appropriate to speak of three types of glory, since there are, in fact, three types of *amores* (i.e., that of the *superbi*, that of the *boni sine fide*, and that of the *sancti*). Augustine's more typical view that all men are governed by one of two *amores* (i.e., *amor sui* or *amor Dei*) and thus preoccupied with one or the other of two types of *gloria* does not easily accommodate a *tertium quid*, but it is clear that there are individuals who fall outside the categories of *sancti* or *superbi* and who practice a kind of natural virtue for which they receive a temporal reward." In the final analysis, temporal glory plays a significant role in encouraging Christian virtue.

59 —_____. "Augustine on War and Killing: Another View." *Harvard Theological Review* **66 (1973), 369-383.**

Swift here responds to Richard S. Hartigan's 1966 article on the same subject published in the *Journal of the History of Ideas.* While he believes that Hartigan "rightly focused on some of the differences inherent in Augustine's views," Swift returns to the original Latin texts for translations and rhetorical analyses that challenge his predecessor's arguments and his "structuring of the problem as a whole." Two key elements of Hartigan's article are disputed: first, the responsibility of the individual soldier to execute an immoral command and, second, the interpretation of Augustine on the fate of the innocent in warfare.

To the former, Swift argues that a subordinate's epistemological problems may be such "that instances of justifiable disobedience in military matters would be rare or virtually nonexistent. But there seems to be enough evidence in Augustine's writing to indicate that he did not endorse the Eichmann mentality." To the latter, Swift argues that it is necessary to "distinguish between subjective and objective guilt." If this distinction "is not recognized, and if, instead, we speak only of guilt in the subjective individual sense as the justification for killing the enemy; if, in short, we equate those combatants who lack a volitional commitment to injustice with noncombatants, just wars would not be 'severely limited'; in any real sense, they would be excluded altogether." The essay also discusses the limits and goals of warfare and the role of mercy as it affects the warrior.

See Hartigan, entry number 26 above.

60 — TeSelle, Eugene. "Toward an Augustinian Politics." *Journal of Religious Ethics* **16 (1988), 87-108.**

In an attempt to clarify Augustine's views on political life, the author traces three lines of reasoning in Augustine's writings. Of these three modes of approach one is a defense of the political viability of the Christian ethic — and of the norms of justice which it shares with classical culture and the Roman political ethos.

Another is a "realistic" interest in describing the disordered affections of sinful humanity and the political processes by which these are harnessed in collective ways. A third looks at the willing of ends, enabling Augustine both to envisage the final values of the city of God and to affirm the values of the earthly city.

The author focuses primarily on Augustine's views as expressed in *The City of God.* The essay concludes that, contrary to the opinion of many contemporary Augustinian scholars, political life for Augustine has positive value. As the author says, "Augustine was not prepared to write off anything human, for it either had some intrinsic goodness (in the case of a being), or was willed for the sake of some value (in the case of objects or projects), or had some social contribution to make (in the case of human institutions); even in perverseness it could attest to some more positive and inclusive value."

**61 — _____. "Civic Vision in Augustine's *City of God.*"
Thought 62 (1987), 268-280.**

According to this study, Augustine's emphasis in *The City of God* is on the *civitas* (the community of citizens), not the *urbs* (the physical setting). Augustine finds two contrary affections, two contrary modes of interaction among purposive beings. The author argues that in the West, the Augustinian tradition has been explicated, in thought and in practice, in several different ways — a passive duality of the two cities, dominated by the City of God, and a cautious affirmation of the finite and changing values of the earthly city.

It is suggested that the most authentic reading of Augustine is a dualistic one, in which the earthly city has only "provisional significance," while the citizens of the "other city live as aliens in its midst and anticipate a fulfillment under very different conditions." The author stresses, however, that Augustine affirms the genuine value of the earthly city, precisely as earthly. The *civitas terrena* has its positive features and necessary role in human history by virtue of the fact that it participates in the fulfillment of God's divine providence.

62 — von Campenhausen, Hans.   "Augustine and the Fall of Rome."   In *Tradition and Life in the Church: Essays and Lectures in Church History*.   Trans. A. V. Littledale. Pennsylvania: Fortress Press, 1968. Pp. 201-216.

This transcription of an inaugural lecture addresses the theological as well as political concerns of *De civitate Dei* in defending Christianity from its detractors following the fall of Rome.   von Campenhausen considers aspects of the work as they are directed toward both pagan and Christian audiences and delineates basic elements of Augustinian philosophy.

Pertaining to politics, the author notes not Augustine's abjuration of political responsibility but "his positive refusal to take the political situation as tragic." Augustine's asceticism and spiritualism — and that of the Christianity of his time — is also set in contrast to Christ and earlier Christianity.   Finally, the debt of modern history to Augustine's concept of salvation-history is briefly discussed.

63 — Watson, Thomas R. *Perversions, Originals, and Redemptions: Typological Patterns Underlining Theme in* Paradise Lost *Based Upon Augustine's* De Civitate Dei.   Dissertation. University of Louisville, 1981.

This work proposes that from the outset Milton, in *Paradise Lost*, follows Augustine's historical scheme as developed in *De civitate Dei*.   To unite his epic internally, and to connect it directly to the Christian tradition, Milton employs the same kinds of figurative patterns found in *De civitate Dei*, "patterns which Augustine based upon his close comparison of the Old and New Testaments." According to the author, the figurative patterns employed by Milton center on two of the main themes dealt with in *The City of God*: first, the idea that only by remaining in communion with God can created beings enjoy the harmony that characterizes *The City of God*; and second, the notion that it is the "proud lifting up of self" in opposition to God which results in the "dark, disharmonious pattern of Satan, from which all sorts of perverse patterns are bred."   In sum, the work proposes that a vast and intricate web of interlocking typological patterns forms the "warp and woof of *Paradise Lost,* much as it has formed the tapestry of *De civitate Dei.*"

64 — Wilson, Everett L. *"The City of God and the Emergence of Christendom." Covenant Quarterly* 42 (1984), 15-26.

The purpose of this article is "to sketch, in rather large summary statements, those ideas in [*The City of God*] which were compatible with the shaping of medieval Christendom." Through a compilation of excerpts from the work itself the author shows how Augustine focuses on three central "affirmations" in *The City of God*—specifically, "nature is good; history has meaning; the Church is the mainstream of history." The essay proposes that *The City of God* "affected the emergence of Christendom" because it is "a primary classic that took the intellectual high ground from the ancients, . . . a comprehensive statement that placed the Church in its natural and historical environment, . . . and it marks a decisive shift from a pagan philosophical base to a Christian theological one in medieval thought."

Part II

Important Earlier Works

65 —Angus, S. *The Sources of the First Ten Books of Augustine's* **De Civitate Dei. New Jersey: Princeton University Press, 1906.**

This important study offers a comprehensive examination of the sources of the first ten books of Augustine's *De civitate Dei*. The work consists of three parts. The first part, "Literary Sources in Books I-X," provides a detailed discussion of all the ascertainable sources, with the exception of the Bible, used by Augustine in Books I-X of *De civitate Dei*. The second part of the work, "Annotations to Books I-X," contains information about Augustine's sources that were not clearly ascertainable and so were not appropriate to the discussion in part one. These two parts are intended to supplement each other. The third part of the study, "Augustine's Knowledge of Greek," describes the extent of Augustine's use of Greek in his writings.

The discussion in part one on Augustine's literary sources reviews both the sources Augustine mentions having known and those he doesn't mention but for which there is evidence to show that he was fully aware of them. Among the sources mentioned by Augustine, we find the names of pagan poets such as Claudian, Ennius, Horace, Lucan, Persius, Teretianus Maurus, Terence, Valerius Soranus, Virgil, and Homer. The prose writers used and named by Augustine include Apuleius, Cicero, Aulus Gellius, Justinus, Labeo, Livy, Plato, Pliny, Plotinus, Pomponius, Porphyry, Sallust, Seneca, Tertullian and Varro. The writers he borrowed from, but whom he does not mention by name, include Florus, Eutropius, Lactantius, and Juvenal. The study notes the specific points in Books I-X where Augustine refers to these writers and cites references to show the way in which Augustine made use of sources.   Part Two, "Annotations to Books I-X," consists of a discussion, again with examples, of the numerous other miscellaneous sources of information used by Augustine throughout Books I-X.

The method used to investigate the question of Augustine's knowledge of Greek is two-fold.   The author examines what Augustine himself says about his knowledge of Greek, on the one hand, and the extent to which Augustine's works show a use of Greek, on the other.   The study concludes that Augustine's knowledge of Greek was imperfect and incomplete.   As the author puts it, "it cannot be described as merely elementary: it was altogether more perfect than his knowledge of it was extensive. . . ."   On the other hand, the author warns, we must not overestimate his knowledge of Greek.   "The fact that he did not employ Greek more . . . shows that his Greek was not very extensive."   Augustine himself claims to have known very little about Greek and his writings reveal that he almost always preferred using a Latin version of a Greek author.

66 — Baynes, Norman H. *The Political Ideas of St. Augustine's* **De Civitate Dei. Historical Association Pamphlet No. 104. London: Bell, 1936. Rpt. in** *Byzantine Studies and Other Essays.* **London: Athlone Press, 1955. Pp. 288-306.**

Originally one of a series of lectures, this essay, first published in 1936, "was designed to form an introduction to the study of the modern literature on the subject of social and political ideals."   But despite its age and the apology that "it raises no claim to originality," as an introduction to the problem of politics in *De civitate Dei* there is a solid foundation to be gotten from this important work. The author sketches Augustine's historical milieu and reviews the possible sources from which he seems to have borrowed the concept of two *civitates* before turning to a study of Augustine's particular use of the term *civitas*.

Proceeding from the basic dualism of Augustine's philosophy, the essay delineates the impact of that issue on the Augustinian notion of the state and its relation to the institutional church. Thence, it explores the roles of the individual person and justice in the state, followed by Augustine's views on, and the origins and natures of, the *civitas terrena* and *civitas Dei*. Finally, it considers some of the misinterpretations of Augustinian political philosophy and their contribution to the medieval ecclesiastical empire. The article starts with the caution, and reasserts it toward the end, against attempts at trying to seek "Augustine's view *as a whole* on any particular [political] subject" primarily because Augustine is in his political theory "no systematic philosopher."

67 — Burleigh, John H. S. The City of God: *A Study of St. Augustine's Philosophy*. **London: Nisbet & Co., 1949.**

This book offers an excellent general introduction to *The City of God*. The author's method is to delineate the arguments made by Augustine in *The City of God* by means of a running commentary on each of the work's twenty-two books. Augustine's statements are first summarized and then compared with the views and attitudes of his predecessors and his contemporaries. In his discussion the author focuses particular attention on those matters that he feels are still issues of theological debate, namely, the relation between religion and philosophy and between church and state.

Chapter one of this study offers a review of the historical circumstances which called forth the writing of *The City of God*. It is pointed out that Augustine, unlike many of his contemporaries, does not despair but, on the contrary, seeks what comfort he can in the calamity that has fallen upon his country. In contrast to the bitter reactions and complaints expressed by many others, Augustine confidently announces in the first book of *The City of God* that his intention is not only to answer anti-Christian propaganda but to set forth a defense of Christianity. According to the essay, a central factor in Augustine's ability to achieve this optimistic point of view is his emphatic rejection of the classical notion of a "utilitarian nexus betwen religion and politics." Unlike Plato and Symmachus, for example, who look to religion for a "final sanction for moral conduct," Augustine is far more committed to the truth of religion than to whatever utilitarian purpose it might have.

Chapter two is devoted to a treatment of the evolution of Augustine's Christian philosophy and traces his indebtedness to earlier writers and their influence upon his thought. The impact upon Augustine of the ideas of Cicero and Ambrose, and the influence of Stoic doctrine and Manicheism, are dealt with. Using Book VIII of *The City of God* as a particular point of reference, the author discusses at length the role of Platonism in Augustinian doctrine. The argument is made that the most important idea Augustine derived from Platonism was the concept of "incorporeal substance; that is to say, a reality (*res*) which is not material." Chapter three continues the discussion of the influence on Augustinian doctrine of earlier writings, with special focus here on the importance of Scripture. Acknowledging Augustine's self-confessed early ignorance of Scripture, the author argues that Augustine, in spite of the fact that he "approaches the Bible with Platonist assumptions," comes to accept Scripture "as the supreme source of saving truth" because it, unlike Platonism, combines both "simplicity and profundity."

In chapter four the author summarizes those Scriptural truths — e.g., the idea of creation, the goodness of created beings, the immortal soul, the doctrine of the fall, etc. — that Augustine came to accept and which he discusses in detail in *The City of God*, especially in Books X-XIII. Within this context, Augustine's plan of salvation, as developed through the conceptualization of the origin, role and purpose of the "two cities," is also touched upon. This section of the work concludes with a discussion of Augustine's ideas about the "blessings of this life." Referring to chapter 24 in Book XXII as a "remarkable chapter," the author claims that this chapter "cannot but astonish us by its unrestrained expression of the *joie de vivre* so unusual in St. Augustine." Even though this sense of joy is not typical of Augustine, it is nonetheless consistent with his belief that, because God created all things, "existence quā existence is good."

Chapters five and six provide a summary of Augustine's social and philosophical ideas. His views on the social and political nature of human beings and his attitude toward the actual political structures of the state are reviewed in chapter five. As in earlier chapters here too the approach is first to present Augustine's ideas as developed in *The City of God* and then to compare them with those of earlier thinkers, in this instance those classical writers who developed ideas about political theory. Special attention is given to the ideas in Book XIX regarding the nature of the state and its relationship to the *civitas terrena*. The main point here is that for

Augustine there is a region "beyond politics" that is superior to the classical ideal state.

In the final chapter the author assesses Augustine's contribution to the philosophy of history and concludes that, while it must be admitted that Augustine is essentially anti-historical in his explanation of human events, he nonetheless develops a comprehensive notion of a Christian universal history, a history that is ordained by divine providence and which follows a divine plan. For Augustine history is the interaction of two universal transpolitical societies — the *civitas terrena* and the *civitas Dei* — which run their course throughout history "concurrently and inseparably."

68 — Carlyle, A. J. "St. Augustine and *The City of God.*" In *The Social and Political Ideas of Some Great Medieval Thinkers.* Ed. F. J. C. Hearnshaw. London: Harrup, 1923.

This article begins with an overview of the historical events and circumstances of the period in which *The City of God* was written and offers a brief summary of Augustine's reasons for writing the work. The main subject of the essay, however, is a discussion of the place of St. Augustine in the history of political theory.

To answer the question about Augustine's political theory, the author reviews earlier conceptions of society and the state, especially the ideas of the Stoic writers. In this he focuses on Seneca's political philosophy and, in turn, on the close similarity between the Stoic theory of the state as the product of a "primitive catastrophe" and the doctrine of the Fall. For the Christians, sin appeared with the "development of vice." The author notes that Seneca's views on the origin of the state are thus shared by all the Christian Fathers, without exception.

The essay shows, however, that while Augustine follows Seneca regarding the *origin* of the state, he departs significantly from his views concerning the question of its ultimate *purpose*. In *De civitate Dei* Augustine very carefully argues that although "the institutions of government have been made necessary by sin, the state is also a divinely appointed remedy for sin." The state, in other words, is derived directly from God and is thus a divinely ordained instrument "by which the graver vices of men may be restrained." The state is not itself "sinful, but rather the remedy for sin." The author disagrees with those who suggest that Augustine looked upon the Church as the earthly representative of the City of God. On the contrary, Augustine did not regard the Church as, in the author's words, "having in its proper nature any kind of relation of authority or supremacy over the State."

On the question of Augustine's views on the relation of the state to justice, the essay strongly argues that if Augustine's challenge, as developed in book 19 of *De civitate Dei*, of Cicero's definition of a true *res publica* is taken seriously then it represents, since it eliminates the concept of justice from the theory of the nature of the state, "a deplorable error for a great Christian teacher." The essay's conclusion on this point is two-fold. On the one hand, Augustine is often ambiguous in his analysis of the relation between justice and the state and we therefore can not know for certain if his views on this matter "represent a settled conviction." On the other hand, the author claims "the matter is not important, for if indeed he did make the mistake it had no significance in the history of Christian ideas." *De civitate Dei* is repeatedly referred to in the Middle Ages but Augustine's separation of justice from the idea of the state is not mentioned.

69 — Dawson, Christopher. "St. Augustine and His Age." In *A Monument to St. Augustine: Essays on Some Aspects of His Thought Written in Commemoration of His 15th Centenary.* Ed. M. C. D'Arcy, et al. London: Sheed and Ward, 1945. Pp. 11-77. First published in 1930.

This extended essay is divided into two parts. The first part, "The Dying World," focuses on the historical events which inspired Augustine to write *The City of God* and proposes that the period in which the work was written was at once a period of material loss and of great religious achievements. The age, the author asserts, "marks the failure of the greatest experiment in secular civilization that the world has ever seen, and the return of society to spiritual principles." The author's purpose in this section is to lay the ground for his discussion of Augustine's treatment of the idea of "two cities" by emphasizing that Christianity was not responsible for the decline of the old world; rather, he argues, "ancient civilization had set itself in opposition to the religious spirit and had alienated the deepest forces in the mind of the age, and thereby its ultimate doom was sealed." From this perspective, *De civitate Dei* is a product of the religious spirit of the period rather than a response to the accusation that Christianity was responsible for the miseries of the world.

The second part of the essay, "The City of God," aims to show that Augustine's work "is the one great work of Christian antiquity which professedly deals with the relation of the state and of human society in general to Christian principles." The author traces the history, in early Christian and Greek thought, of the idea of the "two cities." It is pointed out that the notion of social dualism—i.e., two societies and twofold citizenship—is characteristic of early Christian thought. In its earlier form, this dualism was much more concrete than it afterwards became. It embraced the notion of two opposing orders—the Kingdom of God and the kingdom of this world—which, although they mingled physically, had no spiritual contact. As the author puts it: "There could be no bond of spiritual fellowship or common citizenship between the members of the two societies. In his relations with the state and secular society the Christian felt himself to be an alien—*peregrinus*; his true citizenship was in the Kingdom of Heaven."

Thus Augustine's theme of two cities is for the author not a new discovery. But Augustine's use of the concept significantly departs in its particulars from the ideas put forth by his predecessors and his contemporaries. Augustine is nearer to Tyconius and the early Church Fathers than to Origen, Eusebius, and Tertullian. Origen's speculative theology, Tertullian's uncompromising spirit, Eusebius' ideal sacred monarchy and the fanaticism of the Donatist movement were all too extreme for Augustine. The influence of Tyconius and the Church Fathers is seen above all in Augustine's emphasis on the notion of eschatological and social dualism and in his doctrine of the two cities.

Augustine, like St. Cyprian, believes that the "human race has been vitiated at its source" and that the kingdoms of this world are all "founded in injustice." And, following Tyconius, Augustine holds that humankind has been divided into membership in either one or the other of two cities. It is pointed out, however, that even though Augustine derives the central unifying idea of his work—two cities—from Tyconius "the idea acquired a more profound significance in Augustine's use of the concept than that which Tyconius had given it." To Tyconius, as the author puts it, the two cities were bound up with "realistic eschatological" ideas. To Augustine, on the other hand, they had acquired a philosophic view and had been "related to a rational theory of sociology."

The author concludes that the originality of *De civitate Dei* consists in the fact that "it unites in a coherent system two distinct intellectual traditions which had hitherto proved irreconcilable." The Greeks had a theory of society and a political philosophy but not a philosophy of history. The Christians, on the other hand, had no theory of society or political philosophy but they did have a theory of history. Augustine reconciled these traditions in his theory of universal history based upon the concept of two universal societies which "intermingle" in human history.

70 — Deane, Herbert. *The Political and Social Ideas of St. Augustine.* New York: Columbia University Press, 1963.

The aim of this study is three-fold. First, it is to provide in one work those passages from Augustine's writings in which he discusses the social order and the purpose of the state. The second is to analyze the point of view that permeates Augustine's statements about social and political life. And, finally, the study is a critical commentary on Augustine's social and political doctrines and it attempts to illuminate the relationship between those doctrines and the overall framework of Augustine's thought.

As noted, the author's purpose is to study Augustine's political and social ideas through an analysis of Augustine's comments throughout the whole corpus of his writings. Thus most of the discussion does not deal directly with *The City of God*. It is only in chapter four, "The State: The Return of Order Upon Disorder," that the study focuses on *The City of God*. This section offers a detailed discussion of Book XIX where Augustine challenges the definition of a people (*populus*) and of a commonwealth or state (*res publica*) given by Scipio in Cicero's *De Republica*. It is observed that Augustine rejects Scipio's ideas on justice and the ideal state and that he substitutes in their place a new interpretation of true justice and a new explanation of the role and purpose of the state.

In his analysis the author strongly, and at length, challenges the views of Professor Charles McIlwain who claims that Augustine actually agrees with the Ciceronian definition of the state or *res publica*. He shows that McIlwain disregards, on the one hand, Augustine's redefinition of true justice and, on the other, his alternative definition of a true *res publica* which Augustine proposes as a substitute for the Scipionic definition. According to the author, McIlwain fails to prove that Augustine really accepted Cicero's views on justice and the state. On the contrary, the chapter concludes that for Augustine "the state itself — the political order — can never be truly just."

71 — Deferrari, R. J. and M. J. Keeler. "St Augustine's *City of God*: Its Plan and Development." *American Journal of Philology* 50 (1929), 109-137.

Using *The City of God* and the *Retractations* as their sources, the authors of this article propose to demonstrate that Augustine's original plan for *The City of God* "was actually carried out in the finished masterpiece." The essay also includes a discussion of the work's "defects" — e.g., digressions, repetitions, etc. — that might be thought to "mar the plan."

The essay points out that although Augustine refers to his plan in every book of *The City of God*, it is in Book I, Chs. 35 and 36, Book X, Ch. 32, and Book XVIII, Ch. 1, that his plan is most fully discussed. The study provides a detailed analysis of Augustine's general statements about his plan and the way he carried it out in the chapters and books of *The City of God*. By comparing Augustine's statements from *The City of God* with those found in the *Retractations*, the article is able to show that what Augustine had in mind when he began writing the first book of *The City of God* was practically unchanged fourteen years later when the twenty-two books were completed. In addition, the authors note that Augustine weaves his plan throughout the twenty-two books by repeatedly mentioning topics that will be discussed in subsequent chapters and by referring back to those dealt with in early parts of the work.

Part two of the article presents a table listing the subject matter, by chapter, of the twenty-two books of *The City of God*. According to the article, this table helps to prove that Augustine conformed to his original plan. On the other hand, the table also reveals that Augustine often writes in a "rambling, leisurely style." Accordingly, as the authors put it, "of the 1220 Teubner pages of *The City of God*, about 247 (one fifth of the whole) contain material which has no immediate or essential connection with the subject."

In part three the authors discuss the work's more overt "defects." These are grouped into six classes: 1) digressions, 2) lengthy expositions, 3) superfluous arguments, 4) useless details, 5) repetitions, and 6) overuse of symbolism. Because of these "defects" some of the books in *The City of God* are "much less regularly constructed than others." However, when the twenty-two books as a whole are examined it nonetheless remains that there is "no essential difference between Augustine's proposed plan and his completed work."

72 —Figgis, John Neville. *The Political Aspects of St. Augustine's City of God.* London: Longmans, Green, 1921. Rpt. Massachusetts: Peter Smith, 1963.

Augustine's influence on political thought is the main topic of this early but still important study of *De civitate Dei*. Acknowledging that *De civitate Dei* is not itself a treatise on politics, the author states his intention to study the political thought that is nonetheless embedded in it. He poses the following questions as the framework of his study: 1) Had Augustine a philosophy of history?; 2) Does Augustine condemn the state?; 3) What is Augustine's view of the place of the Church in relation to civil society?; 4) What was Augustine's influence on the Middle Ages?; 5) Has Augustine's social doctrine lost all influence?

Before turning to a discussion of these specific questions, the author offers in an extended introductory chapter a review of the general scope of *De civitate Dei*. For each book of Augustine's "masterpiece," he summarizes the ideas presented and the main arguments Augustine offers in defense of his views. At several important points the author takes care to show the connection between the ideas developed in later books of *De civitate Dei* and those presented in preceding ones. Finally, the introductory chapter concludes with the observation that, as the review presented in this study makes clear, *De civitate Dei* is, and was intended to be, "apologetic and theological."

The author answers in turn each of the questions that frame this work. In response to question one, according to the author, Augustine, even though he did not set out to articulate a philosophy of history, was most certainly historically minded. Through his conceptualization of the two cities, he dealt with the importance of human history and its relation to a sphere beyond the temporal world. Augustine's philosophy of history is thus a "philosophy of the time-process as a whole." In reply to the second question, this study points out that, for Augustine, the term *civitas* is not synonymous with the state, rather, it is equivalent to society. For Augustine, human beings are by nature social and the primary distinction he makes is between two different kinds of universal societies. Unlike the Donatists, who regarded the state as a profane institution, Augustine argues that the state, however flawed it may be, is nonetheless a divine necessity and therefore good.

The question of the place of the church in civil society is taken up next. Citing passages from Book XX of *De civitate Dei*, the author proposes that the notion of the church as a "social entity wielding governing powers owes much to S. Augustine." In Augustine's time, the church was not equal in power to civil authority. However, Augustine's ideas about the civil and religious authorities as co-ordinate powers in the state became increasingly influential and reached fruition in the Middle Ages. A world governed by Pope and Emperor became a medieval ideal, albeit one surrounded by great controversy. In this debate there was an almost total dependence upon Augustine's political and theological views among those who supported the dual political arrangement.

Although the impact of *De civitate Dei* declined when the medieval unity broke up, Augustine's social ideas have remained significant, according to the author. The influence of *De civitate Dei* he believes is seen today not so much in particular political systems but rather in the example it provides of the struggle to achieve the ideal. The author concludes that in addition to its continuing theological significance, and apart from the importance of its political comments, the lasting impact of *De civitate Dei* derives from its representation of the individual and collective search for higher ideals.

73 — Marshall, R. T. *Studies in the Political and Socio-Religious Terminology of the* **De Civitate Dei.** **Washington, D. C.: Catholic University Press, 1952.**

Any meaningful interpretation of the central theme of *De civitate Dei* depends upon a full understanding of what Augustine means by the two cities — *civitas Dei* and *civitas terrena*. This study proposes to meet this need by examining the "all-important term," *civitas*, as well as other major collective terms used by Augustine in *De civitate Dei* — specifically, *populus, gens, regnum, societas,* and *res publica*. The method is to cite the frequency of use of the terms under consideration and to compare and contrast their usage to determine Augustine's meaning. The essay provides a discussion of the distinctions among the major terms under consideration and the other kinds of "collective" terms used by Augustine. Also included are several tables showing comprehensive lists of all relevant uses of the particular term under discussion, including the use of equivalents which indicate a distinctly different use of the term.

The underlying premise of the study is that the *De civitate Dei* is, in the author's words, "essentially a social document; that is, it considers man not as an individual, but as a member or element of an organized collectivity." And the *civitas Dei* and the *civitas terrena* are "social collectivities" which are "more inclusive in their membership" than, for example, the Greek *polis*. The author points out that the term *societas* is "completely interchangeable with *civitas* as used in reference to the two great *civitates*."

The term *civitas*, however, also has a political meaning in the *De civitate Dei*. Actually, the term has, according to the author, three distinct meanings: 1) an all-comprehensive collectivity — e.g., *civitas Dei*; 2) a limited collectivity — e.g., *civitas Romana*; and 3) a municipal collectivity — e.g., *civitas Carthago*. The author argues that the meanings attached to the last two examples are commonplace in Latin. It is in applying *civitas* to the two universal societies — the *civitas terrena* and the *civitas Dei* — that Augustine goes beyond the ordinary meanings associated with the term *civitas*. The study concludes with a general discussion of the relation of other *civitates* to each other, the relation between *civitas Dei* and *ecclesia*, and the relation between the *civitas terrena* and the state.

See Adams, entry number 1 above.

74 — Mommsen, Theodor E. "Orosius and Augustine." In *Medieval and Renaissance Studies.* **Ed. Eugene F. Rice, Jr. New York: Cornell University Press, 1959. Pp. 325-348.**

The purpose of this study is to investigate through a close textual analysis the claim that Orosius' *Seven Books of History Against the Pagans* supplied the essential material for Augustine's *City of God.* The author intends to show that the medieval opinion, "still maintained by most modern scholars," that the *Seven Books* offers an interpretation of history from the Augustinian point of view is based upon several erroneous assumptions. In fact, the differences between the two works are far greater than is generally recognized.

A comparison of Orosius' *Seven Books* with the first part of *The City of God* does show a similarity in the way the theme of "material calamity" is handled by the two authors. In both there is a preoccupation with the material evils of this world and a lack of emphasis on the spiritual and ethical concerns of humankind. The essay argues, however, that when the two works are compared in their entirety one essential difference becomes immediately evident. Augustine's purpose was to "discuss fully 'the origin, the course, and the end of the two cities,' especially of the heavenly city," whereas Orosius' aim was to "tell the tale of human misery in history." In brief, Orosius' preoccupation was with the temporal or earthly city whereas Augustine's primary concern was with the eternal or heavenly city.

The article discusses several other points which, it is proposed, reveal the significant divergence of opinion in the *Seven Books* and *The City of God.* For example, Orosius' analysis of the course of human history in the *Seven Books* leads him to find "a definite pattern of progress made by mankind with the help of the Christian God." Orosius thus placed himself in the tradition of the "Christian progressivists." This interpretation of history is based upon "principles most explicitly rejected by Augustine in *The City of God.*" Another significant difference of opinion derives from Orosius' acceptance of the ancient notion of history as a succession of "four main kingdoms, pre-eminent in successive stages at the four cardinal points of the earth." In contrast, at no point in *The City of God* does Augustine "ever mention in any explicit way the scheme of the four great monarchies." The author concludes that in spite of their similarities, *Seven Books of History Against the Pagans* and *The City of God* offer radically different interpretations of the purpose and destiny of human history.

75 — _____. "St. Augustine and the Christian Idea of Progress. The Background of *The City of God*." *Journal of the History of Ideas* 12 (1952), 346-374. Rpt. in *Medieval and Renaissance Studies*. Ed. Eugene F. Rice, Jr. New York: Cornell Univ. Press, 1959. Pp. 265-298.

This extended analysis of Augustine's interpretation of the meaning and course of history concludes that he rejects both the cyclical theory proposed by the Platonists and the Stoics and the early Christian proposition that real temporal progress could be observed from the Incarnation onward. In addition to the cyclical theories of the Greeks, Augustine rejected as an equally deplorable theory of history the Christian idea of "progress." In his theological explanation of the meaning of history, Augustine thus rejects the view that the world is eternal and the notion that human history is accompanied by evolutionary progress. To Augustine, history is linear, not cyclical. And in his view the notion of Christianity as a progressive factor in history is contrary to God's divine plan.

The author points out that examples of the expression of the idea of progression can be found in many early Christian writings. For example, in his *Apology* addressed to Emperor Antoninus Pius, Bishop Melito of Sardis voices the view that under Christianity the world had seen great "progress in historical time and that further progress could be expected." Tertullian expressed similar views in his *Apology*: "And for all that is said, if we compare the calamities of former times [with those of our own era], we find that they fall on us more lightly now, since the earth has received from God the believers of the Christian faith." In addition to Melito and Tertullian, the belief that the acceptance of Christianity will lead to greater progress was also set forth by Origen, Arnobius, and Lactantius. But the most important figure in postulating the idea of progress was Eusebius. According to the essay, "there was no doubt in Eusebius' mind that mankind, under divine guidance, had made progress from the pre-Christian era through the three centuries of the gradual ascent of the new Church to the reign of Constantine in which he himself lived. . . . And still further progress was expected by Eusebius." It is pointed out that Eusebius' idea was accepted by most fourth-and early fifth-century theologians.

The author argues that Augustine emphatically rejected the principle of progress as an important factor in human history. In Augustine's view, Christian ideals can be realized only in the spiritual community of God not in the temporal state or empire. He regards the so-called "earthly achievements" as totally insignificant. Not surprisingly, Augustine condemns his worldly-minded Christian contemporaries as "blasphemers who chase and long after things earthly and place their hopes in things earthly. When they have lost them, whether they will or not, what shall they hold and where shall they abide? Nothing within, nothing without; an empty coffer, an emptier conscience."

The essay concludes that in *De civitate Dei* Augustine rejects practically all the conceptions of history proposed by his contemporaries and by his predecessors. He rejects the view of the imminence of the end of the world, eschews the cyclical theory of history, dismisses eschatological speculation regarding the future millennium, and denies the doctrine of progress. The author claims that "in contradistinction to all these conceptions, Augustine's own views concerning history represent a basic reiteration and systematic elaboration of Hebrew and early Christian ideas."

76 — Rickaby, Joseph. *St. Augustine's* **City of God:** *A View of the Contents*. **London: Burns Oates & Washbourne, 1925.**

This work offers a study of the contents of each of the twenty-two books of *De civitate Dei*. Two extended appendices are also included. Appendix I is "Natural Wonders, As They Appeared in St. Augustine's Time," and Appendix II is "A List of Miracles, Coming Under St. Augustine's Own Notice."

In his analysis of Augustine's political views, the author focuses on Augustine's treatment of the ends of the two cities within the context of Augustine's concept of happiness, his attitude toward war, his explanation of "natural virtues," his definition of peace, and his challenge of Cicero's views on justice. The author observes that, for Augustine, "the Two Cities are not the Church and the World, but the Elect and the Reprobate." And in his discussion of this idea he stresses the following related points: 1) "The Elect and the Reprobate do not form two visible societies on earth"; 2) "The Elect and the Reprobate live side by side and together make up the Church on earth"; 3) "These Two Cities are together in this world, till they are parted at the Last Judgment."

The author's method in each of the commentaries is to compare Augustine's ideas with the views of his contemporaries and his predecessors. Augustine's opinions and comments are also discussed in relation to their historical situation.

77 — Versfeld, Marthinus. *A Guide to* The City of God. New York: Sheed and Ward, 1958.

This work aims to serve as a "guide" to the "mind of Augustine" through a close textual analysis of the ideas put forth in *The City of God*. The work deals with the last twelve books of *The City of God*. The author omits Books I-X because, on the one hand, they are "too negative and polemical" and, on the other, "many of the controversies raised in them are as dead as these things ever become." The author's overall method is to offer a chapter-by-chapter analysis of Augustine's text in the course of which Augustine's leading principles and main arguments are isolated for purposes of clarification.

The work, as the author puts it, "passes lightly" over Books XV, XVI, XVII, and XVIII, and only briefly deals with Books XX-XXII. Its real focus is on a comprehensive analysis of the idea of the "two cities" as presented by Augustine in Book XIX. The author claims that "it is the peace of the *civitas terrena*, of a body without life, in which has been bred the new and supernatural life." From this point of view, the *civitas terrena* is good, but this "in no way mitigates the sentence of damnation." There is a certain common ground between the *civitas terrena* and the *civitas Dei* which derives from the fact that everything participates in God's universal scheme of peace and order. Thus although the ends of the two cities are different they nonetheless find a *modus communiter vivendi*.

In a lengthy "Appendix to the Analysis of Book XIX," the author discusses the relationship between Augustine's thought and Platonic idealism. Special attention is given to the religious element in Plato's philosophy. For Plato too there is the notion of a "Presence as a source of grace, the grace which above all human possibility (*Repub.*, vi) rescues the philosopher from the self-centered life." And in Platonic thought there are two cities, "the cities of the philosopher and of the philodoxer. The contrast takes the form in the *Republic* of the contrast between the waking and the dreaming lives. . . ." Finally, the author suggests that Augustine inherited a "prison or cave complex" from Plato . . . which prevented him from fully developing his ideas concerning the "consequences of the doctrine of the Incarnation."

Part III

Selected Foreign Studies

78 — Boeft, J. Den. "Some Etymologies in Augustine's *De Civitate Dei* X." *Vigiliae Christianae* 33 (1979), 242-259.

The intent of this study is to show how one of Augustine's rhetorical tools served him in his philosophical disputation with paganism. Given Augustine's belief that (Neo-) Platonism most approximated the Christian faith, the author elucidates the manner in which Augustine's excellence in the classical *ars rhetorica* showed that "the goal to which Porphyry was vainly seeking, viz. liberation of the soul, is in reality the heavenly kingdom, and thus it is again shown how near paganism, in this case Porphyry, was to the truths of Christianity."

To support his argument the author considers in detail Augustine's unique employment of five terms in *De civitate Dei* X: *religio*, *curia*, *res divina*, and *heros* from the pagan tradition, and *via regalis* ultimately derived from *Numbers* 20.17. The study concludes that "these rhetorical etymologies of pagan terms and, in a somewhat different but comparable way, the etymological use of the expression *via regalis*, have in fact the same purpose as the description and discussion of some (Neo-) Platonic doctrines in books VIII-X, viz. to show how near paganism really is to the Christian truths."

79 — Booth, E. "A Marginal Comment of St. Augustine on the Principle of the Division of Labor (*De Civ. Dei* VII, 4)." *Augustiniana* 17 (1977), 249-256.

The passage in question is cited as a rare instance in *De civitate Dei* where Augustine refers to contemporary socioeconomic crises and combines these elements "into a conceptual unit [which] anticipates Adam Smith's articulation of the principles of the divi-

sion of labour." At the same time, however, the essay places
Augustine's comments in historic context in order that we "not
push the comparison too far," on the one hand, and on the other to
present Augustine's view as reaffirming the interrelation of the
commonplace and the eternal.

80 — Burt, Donald X. "St. Augustine's Evaluation of Civil Society." *Augustinianum* 3 (1963), 87-94.

In this essay civil society refers to the state. The author maintains that in Augustine's view the state is "a gift of nature not the
result of sin." For Augustine, "union in civil society is natural to
man." According to the author, this interpretation is underscored
by Augustine's stress on the relationship of the family to the state.
"No one can question the fact that Augustine considers the family
to be a natural society." It is acknowledged that many scholars
have interpreted Augustine's position to be that the state is actually due to the "failure of nature."

This study insists, however, that Augustine's aim in *De civitate
Dei* is "not to destroy the state but to purify it." Augustine's
approach to demonstrating that the state is a "gift of nature" is by
means of an analysis of human nature: "In his general principles
regarding the dignity, purpose, and destiny of the state, [Augustine]
enunciates facts rooted in man's nature."

81 — Carlson, Charles P., Jr. "The Natural Order and Historical Explanation in St. Augustine's *City of God*." *Augustiniana* 21 (1971), 417-447.

It is the intent of this study to restore Augustine's reputation as a
philosopher of history. The article re-examines Augustine's concept of nature with a view toward modifying the long-standing
shadow of Platonism that shaped opinion on the Augustinian attitude toward the physical world, and to show how this view was
integrated into Augustine's thought "by means of historical synthesis" resulting in several important contributions to western historiography.

The author insists that Augustine "did not take his Platonism
whole and go over to a position of extreme idealism." The natural

world, as the product of divine creation, is necessarily good. Thus "substance is not intrinsically evil," it can only be put to misuse by the individual will. And so evil as such exists outside of the natural order. Furthermore, Augustine's retention of "the basic naturalistic modes of explanation of an earlier and greater scientific era" in a world largely given over to popular superstition assumes considerable cultural significance. This is not to suggest, however, that his scientific intellectualism was not subordinate to "his overall sense of values" but, rather, that the result of his labors is a universal history uncommon for his era.

The essay concludes that Augustine's most important contribution to intellectual advancement is his supplanting of the Platonic "cyclic" theory of eternally recurrent time with a linear concept which agrees with Christian eschatology and the concept of temporal finitude. Emerging from this is an affirmation of the "existence and importance of the conventional spatial-temporal continuum of objective history." In Augustine's historical construct the course of history proceeds according to an "objective and recognizable ordering of the universe," and the study of history is an "empirical demonstration of this order."

82 – Clark, Mary T. "Platonic Justice in Aristotle and Augustine." *The Downside Review* **82 (1964), 25-35.**

This article examines the metamorphosis of the Platonic idea of justice into the form which Augustine received and the subsequent impact it had on *De civitate Dei*. Other than Plotinus, the intermediaries for Augustine would have been Aristotle, with his own emerging concept of justice in the *Protrepticus* and the *Eudemian* and *Nichomachean Ethics*, and Cicero's *De republica* and the lost *Hortensius* which "profoundly affected" Augustine by its reproduction of the *Protrepticus*. The author claims that, regarding justice, Augustine has more in common with the young Aristotle than with Plato's "radical dualism."

The Aristotelian definition of a community as "an association of many persons seeking a determined end" is very close to Augustine's communal foundation of common love. That type of friendship has a more fundamental role in the establishment of a just community than merely defining the community as the fruit of justice — as it is for Plato in the *Republic*. This is an important distinction for Aristotle and Augustine. And by seeing passion as subservient to, yet participating with, reason in maintaining justice as the highest and interiorized virtue of an individual or community Augustine embraces other important ideas proposed by Aristotle.

The essay concludes, however, with the caution that we not assume "that the Augustinian development of justice is chiefly Aristotelian." The article "only shows that Augustine seems to follow the thinking of the young Aristotle, and the very early works of Aristotle were modelled both nominally and really on the Platonic dialogues."

83 — Currie, H. MacL. "Saint Augustine and Virgil." *Proceedings of the Virgil Society* 14 (1974-1975), 6-16.

Augustine's conversion to Christianity was not only spiritual but academic as well. "The Scriptures, whose style he had previously found barbarous, became his chief study and delight"; however, what the essay argues is that Augustine never abandoned "his favourite author, Virgil." Virgil stood as a Roman cultural paradigm "of formative intellectual influence upon the young Augustine." In sum, Augustine owes many of his basic philosophical assumptions to Virgil.

The most obvious similarity is Augustine's vision of *De civitate Dei* as "the Christian prose epic of Rome." Throughout *De civitate Dei* the Virgilian presence is "palpable." For example, in considering the question of immortality, Augustine continually refers to Virgil's treatment of the subject in the famous passage on "metempsychosis and purification at *Aeneid* 6. 703ff." Augustine's artistic analysis of time, eternity, history, and progress, as well as his views on war and peace as necessary depravities are seen as dependent upon the great Roman poet. The author concludes that "in their attitude to the *genus humanum*, Augustine and Virgil are not dissimilar."

84 – Dyson, R. W. "St. Augustine's Remarks on Time." *The Downside Review* **100 (1982), 221-230.**

Noting that Augustine's commentators generally refer to his concept of time as singular the author examines *Confessiones* XI, x, 12-xxx, 40 and *De civitate Dei* XI, 4-8 to reveal that Augustine, perhaps unknowingly, developed "not only two theories, but two *incompatible* theories of time." In defending the Christian account of creation *ex nihilo* against the pagan contentions that matter is eternal and God therefore a craftsman in time Augustine proposes a "relational theory" of time, that is, the idea that time is itself a creature of God. In contrast, when he considers what is implied by saying that time exists, Augustine adopts the view that time is "ideal," a subjective extension of the mind over our erroneous denomination of past, present, and future, as opposed to an objective, "real" time theory.

85 – Ferrari, Leo C. "Some Surprising Omissions from Augustine's *City of God.***"** *Augustiniana* **21 (1970), 336-346.**

Three elements not found in *The City of God* are here analyzed historically to reconstruct the motivation for certain omissions from Augustine's treatise. The first omission cited is the "almost complete absence of any kindly concessions towards paganism." A second "surprising omission" is found in the fact that earlier Christian thinkers are rarely discussed in *The City of God* whereas writers in the pagan tradition – Cicero, Virgil, Varro, and Sallust – are frequently mentioned. Another surprising omission concerns "the personality of Christ." Augustine's emphasis in *The City of God* is upon the prophecies which anticipate Christ's coming rather than the "actual words of Christ." Little consideration is given to the physical existence of Christ. "His whole life of thirty three years on earth is abruptly dismissed in a few lines." The author offers some tentative reasons in an attempt to explain these omissions. The explanations provided are primarily historical in nature.

86 — Gibson, Margaret. "Lanfranc's Notes on Patristic Texts."
The Journal of Theological Studies 22 (1971), 435-450.

Presented here for the first time are the edited marginal notes, in Latin, of the eleventh-century *magister* on the *De civitate Dei* and the *Moralia* of Gregory the Great. As the editor notes, "the notes are brief and often puzzling: but they do seem to be a coherent (though very incomplete) textual exegesis." The importance of these notes is the innovative experiment they present of applying the academic methodology of the *artes* to Christian texts: "a courageous, if unsuccessful, experiment." The editor also provides a thorough survey of MSS as well as critical analysis of the collected marginalia.

87 — Gorman, Michael M. "A Survey of the Oldest Manuscripts of St. Augustine's *De Civitate Dei*." *The Journal of Theological Studies* 33 (1982), 398-410.

This article, as the author states, provides "a basis for future research." It is primarily concerned with two matters: the listing of known manuscripts and fragments of *De civitate Dei* produced until the twelfth century and an inconclusive inquiry into the origin of the *capitula* for *De civitate Dei*. The impetus for this compilation is the "very random sample of the oldest manuscripts" used to prepare the Dombart-Kalb edition, the source for current standard editions of *De civitate Dei*. The author's hope is that examination of the manuscripts he surveys will yield further knowledge about the transmission of *De civitate Dei*. The article concludes with the suggestion that Eugippius, a scholar in the monastery of St. Severin in Naples in the sixth century, may be the author of the *capitula* for the work.

88 — Jones, B. V. E. "The Manuscript Tradition of St. Augustine's *De Civitate Dei*." *The Journal of Theological Studies* 16 (1965), 142-145.

After reading an unedited version of a letter from Augustine to an African priest named Firmus, first published in 1939, and after examining MSS of *De civitate Dei* in the British Museum and the

Bodleian Library, it is the author's conclusion that Augustine intended two MS versions of *De civitate Dei*: one of two-volumes and another of five. As evidenced by the letter to Firmus, the "twofold manuscript tradition" was part of Augustine's original plan. Thus some of the apparently "'odd' books" compiled in extant MSS "now begin to make sense and we can begin to classify them."

89 — Markus, Robert A. *"Saeculum": History and Society in the Theology of Saint Augustine.* **Cambridge: Cambridge University Press, 1970.**

The central focus of this valuable study is on two interrelated themes — Augustine's view of human history and the role of divine providence in that history and his view of the purpose of human society in relation to the individual's ultimate other-worldly destiny. In discussing these themes the author deals with Augustine's ideas as they are expressed in the entire corpus of his writings. Thus the discussion of *The City of God* is developed within the context of other Augustinian writings and is dispersed throughout the text of this study. There are two chapters, however, which, although they too include references to many other works by Augustine, focus more centrally on the particular themes developed in *The City of God* — chapter three, "Civitas Terrena," and chapter four, "*Ordinata est res publica.*"

Chapter three explores the relationship between *The City of God* and the idea that the Roman Empire had a messianic mission. The view of history held by many of Augustine's contemporaries embraced the notion of Rome as the "culmination of God's marvellous saving work." Although Augustine temporarily shared this view, it is clear that by the time he wrote *The City of God* he had repudiated the attempt to "interpret Roman history in prophetic categories." God's plan, he believed, cannot be dependent upon the fate of any temporal state. Thus, in Augustine's hands, as the author puts it, "the Roman Empire has lost its religious significance."

The last section of chapter three offers an insightful analysis of the Augustinian notion of the two cities and the relationship between the *civitas terrena* and the state. It is argued that Augustine views human history as a conflict between the *civitas terrena* and the *civitas Dei*, not between one or the other of these two societies and the state. In book XIX, ch. 17, for example, Augustine makes it clear that in human history "the sphere of politics . . . is autonomous." Politics belongs to the sphere of secular history and for Augustine the only true history is sacred history. In Augustine's thought the difference between secular and sacred history depends on the source of the narrative, that is, whether or not the historical narrative is prophetically inspired. As the author says, "inspiration . . . is the constitutive difference between 'sacred' and 'secular' history."

Turning to chapter four, the author analyzes Augustine's positions on political theory and observes that Augustine's views in this area are almost always implicit rather than explicit. And even those opinions that are explicit do not constitute what could be called a body of political thought. On the contrary, most of what can be concluded about Augustine's political ideas is, in fact, "drawn from what he has to say on other, though related matters." Rejecting the classical theory of the state, a theory which proposed that the means of achieving human perfection in the secular world was through a political system, Augustine focused his comments regarding political and social order on the ideas found in the Judaeo-Christian traditions. From this perspective, the members of the *civitas Dei* could not conceivably think of themselves as active participants in establishing a social political order. "Their whole tradition," according to the author, "was dominated by the need to adjust themselves to a society radically alienated from the one ultimately acceptable form of social existence." For Augustine human societies are societies in which the members of the *civitas Dei* are strangers.

Yet, there is in Augustinian thought a reconciliation with the notion of a proper role and function for the state and this view derives from his hierarchical concept of order. In this scheme, political order is bound up with the notion of an order which pervades the entire universe from the highest transcendent level to the lowest temporal level. Thus social or political institutions in Augustine's view have their proper and legitimate place in human affairs because they are part of a scheme of cosmic order. Political structures are justified because they ensure temporal order which is itself part of a divinely ordained cosmological order. To sum up, in the author's words, "Augustine's conception of the *saeculum* made it possible for politics to resume some of the significance of which his attack on the Platonic tradition (in which politics had *ultimate* significance) had deprived it."

The work includes two appendices which deal directly with the *De civitate Dei*. Appendix B is entitled "*De civitate Dei*, XIX, 14-15 and the Origins of Political Authority." Appendix C deals with "Augustine and the Aristotelian Revolution of the Thirteenth Century." Both appendices were originally published as one paper in *The Journal of Theological Studies*.

See entry number 90 below.

90 – _____. "Two Conceptions of Political Authority: Augustine, *De Civitate Dei*, XIX, 14-15, and Some Thirteenth Century Interpretations." *The Journal of Theological Studies* 16 (1965), 68-100. Rpt. in Robert A. Markus. *"Saeculum": History and Society in the Theology of Saint Augustine*. Cambridge: Cambridge University Press, 1970.

This extended study consists of two parts. The first part examines Augustine's views on the origins and nature of political authority and subjection as presented in Book XIX, chapters 14 and 15, of *De civitate Dei*. The second part discusses the interpretation of these chapters by some thirteenth-century writers, primarily Thomas Aquinas. Among other things, the analysis enables us to see how Augustine's meaning was modified by thirteenth-century thinkers whose ideas were influenced by the revival of Aristotelian thought.

The essay begins with the acknowledgment that Augustine does not develop in any of his writings a detailed theory about the origin of the state. His fullest remarks on the theme occur in *De civitate Dei*, chapters 14 and 15. The author gives a summary of the main topics of these chapters—earthly peace and eternal peace, authority and obedience (*imperare-obedire*) and the origin and nature of servitude. It is proposed that Augustine emphasizes essentially two things in chapters 14 and 15: first, that "servitude is a condition or institution whose origin is not to be found in man's nature as created"; and, second, that "there is a way of exercising authority — and subjection — either in accordance with the order of nature or otherwise." Servitude itself originates in sin "but the exercise of authority need not be sinful." The article notes that a close reading of the text reveals that the two chapters say nothing at all about "the state and political authority . . . as institutions of nature."

For Augustine, a desire for "a harmonious social existence" is natural to human beings. There is also, according to Augustine, "a natural subordination among people," on the one hand, and on the other a "subordination which has its origins in the punishment of sin." The key to understanding Augustine's attitude toward the state and political authority is to understand how he "distinguished natural from non-natural forms of subjection . . . and whether political institutions belong with those of the family [natural] or, rather, with slavery [non-natural]." The author concludes that Augustine's views on the state and political authority were those which he associated with the institution of slavery rather than those of the human family.

In Augustinian thought a social existence is natural; the state is brought into human society by sin. The state is at once a punishment for sin and God's instrument for human redemption. As the author puts it, "political authority, coercive power and its apparatus are what transform society into a state. Society, as we may summarize Augustine's view, has its origins in the order of nature; the state is a dispensation rooted in sin."

The purpose of the second section of the essay is to discuss how Augustine's views on the origin of the state and on political authority were treated by St. Bonaventure, St. Albert the Great, and St. Thomas Aquinas. Of the three writers, Bonaventure's ideas are closest to those of Augustine. Like Augustine, Bonaventure regards political authority "as a human institution sanctioned by a dispensation of divine providence, but not as an ordinance of nature." In contrast, the ideas presented by Albert in his *Summa* reveal that he accepted many of the themes presented by Aristotle in his *Politics*. As the author notes, "by the time he came to write his *Summa*, Albert had come to see the human society in Aristotelian terms." Drawing upon both the Augustinian and Aristotelian traditions, Albert followed Augustine in his views on slavery, Aristotle in his views on politics.

In contrast to Albert, who was content with what is described as a "perfunctory and superficial reconciliation," Aquinas attempted to achieve a synthesis of the Augustinian and Aristotelian traditions within a single unifying framework. Initially, he attempted to deal with the question of political authority, as the author puts it, by "distinguishing two 'modes' of authority: one for the sake of government (*ad regimen ordinatus*), the other for the sake of domination (*ad dominandum*)." Later, however, Aquinas came to accept the Aristotelian doctrine that social existence and political existence are one. In turn, he altered his views on authority. Rather than two modes of authority distinguished by the way authority is exercised, the contrast now, it is argued, is between "authority as existing in slavery and authority as existing, among other institutions, in the 'office of governing free men.' " As the essay indicates, Aquinas had earlier "sought to reconcile Augustine and Aristotle by dividing political authority. . . . Now he treats political authority as all of a piece; and it belongs to the institutions grounded in nature." Unlike Augustine, Aquinas proposes that political society is, like a family, a natural institution.

91 — McCallin, Joseph A.   "The Christological Unity of St. Augustine's *De Civitate Dei.*"   *Revue des études augustiniennes* 12 (1966), 85-109.

The intent of this study is to show how Augustine's use of numbers in *De civitate Dei* gives a unity to the work that is basically Christological. The essay argues that it is only through an understanding of Augustine's use of numbers that a true understanding of the work is revealed. For example, according to the author, "the very form and figure of the Crucified Christ and the Apocalptic Temple . . . shine forth by the use of number in the conduct of the book itself."

The article begins with a lengthy discussion of the general character and purpose of *De civitate Dei*. The well-known historical circumstances and situation, as discussed by Augustine in books one through ten, are briefly recapitulated, and the contents of books eleven through twenty-two are treated in substantial detail.

In this overall description of *De civitate Dei*, however, the author purposefully draws the reader's attention to the presence and symbolic use of number. For example, he points out that in Augustine's numerology, the number five refers to perfection in the Earthly City; the number ten refers to the perfection of justice and beautitude and, taken by itself, "signifies the leit-motif, the Heavenly City."

Through his systematic examination of Augustine's use of number, the author concludes that the numbers three and four reveal the "Trinitarian and evangelical nature of the second part of *De civitate Dei*. That the numbers five, six, ten, and twelve signify the cruciform Body of Christ in the thought and structure of *De civitate Dei* itself is derivable from Augustine's own words." The *De civitate Dei* is thus not integrated only by its logical and rhetorical unity. More importantly, according to this essay, it is unifed by a theological unity revealed by Augustine's extensive and subtle use of number. Based upon an examination of the use of number in *De civitate Dei*, the author concludes that throughout the work, "the form of the City of God itself is the form of the Crucified Christ."

92 — Russell, Robert. "The Role of Neoplatonism in St. Augustine's *The City of God*." In *Neoplatonism and Early Christian Thought*. Ed. Henry J. Blumenthal and Robert A. Markus. London: Variorum Publications, 1981. Pp. 160-170.

Augustine's generally positive attitude towards Platonism is reviewed in this study. But his eventual departure from many of the Platonists' views is the main concern of this essay. The study notes that while Augustine accepts the Platonists' "natural philosophy and dialectic which viewed God, respectively, as the cause of the universe and the source of man's intellectual illumination," his primary concern in *The City of God* is to refute those Platonic "errors" that were incompatible with revealed truth. This study demonstrates that, in discussing this incompatibility, Augustine focuses upon two fundamental Platonic ideas that are at variance with Christian religion — namely, the notion of beautitude and the doctrine of mediatorship.

Plato locates the cause of beautitude in the "transcendent Good or One"; however, Plato's doctrine of eternal cycles, according to the author, "eliminates what was for Augustine the one condition without which true happiness remains incompatible, namely, that it is *unending*." The Platonic view of happiness as a temporary state is linked to the notion that souls are destined to return to other bodies. For Augustine, however, true happiness, which is explained according to the doctrine of the resurrection, is achievable precisely because immortal bodies can share in the eternal happiness of the soul.

Turning to the subject of mediatorship, the author shows that in Book X of *The City of God* Augustine attacks Porphyry's doctrine of mediatorship by focusing on two points: 1) "no philosophy can represent itself as the 'truest philosophy' (*verissima philosophia*) if it merely identifies the goal of man's happiness but fails to provide him with a clear vision of the way to reach that goal"; and 2) "Porphyry's . . . [notion] of theurgy as a means of moral purification . . . is, on Porphyry's own admission, a practice incapable of achieving *complete* purification of the soul." For Augustine, the only way to achieve personal salvation is through Christ. Any theory that proposed a mediator other than that of Christ was, as the author says, "reason enough to turn Augustine against that philosophy."

Augustine found in Platonism a philosophy which lent itself to a rational explanation of revealed truth. Writing as an apologist for Christianity in *The City of God*, however, Augustine felt compelled to show "not where Platonism succeeded, but where it had *failed*."

93 — van der Horst, P. W. "A Pagan Platonist and a Christian Platonist on Suicide." *Vigiliae Christianae* 25 (1971), 282-288.

As the title suggests, this article contrasts the views of two contemporaneous thinkers on suicide, despite their similarities as Platonists. To accomplish this, van der Horst lists the essential arguments in Augustine's *De civitate Dei*, I, 17-27 and Macrobius's *Commentary on the Dream of Scipio*, I, 13. His conclusion is that Macrobius decries suicide "because it is an *unreasonable* act, caused by passions" and as such the soul retains a degree of corporeality making it unable to ascend to the heavens. Augustine, on the other hand, as a Christian, condemns suicide "because it is a *sin*, a transgression of God's prohibition."

94 — van Eijk, A. H. C. " 'Only That Can Rise Which Has Previously Fallen': The History of a Formula." *The Journal of Theological Studies* 22 (1971), 517-529.

The variant interpretations of the formula noted in the title reflects the debate on resurrection in the early centuries of Christianity. The author traces the course of the formula and its attendant heretical and orthodox interpretations from its first appearance in the apocryphal Epistle of the Apostles to Augustine's final word on the matter in *De civitate Dei*, XX, 7-10.

The controversy has to do with whether or not the resurrection of both Christ and the faithful is that of the flesh, the spirit, or both flesh and spirit, and when in time those resurrections occur. Before Augustine, the topic is filtered through the commentary of Justin Martyr, Ignatius of Antioch, Tertullian, Origen, and Methodius. Augustine reinterprets Revelation 20.1-6 in order to distinguish the first death and resurrection, that of the soul, from the second "*quae non nunc, sed in saeculi fine futura est, nec animarum, sed corporum est.*" In the author's opinion, Augustine is critical of the traditional use of the formula, overcomes "a one-sidedness in the ecclesiastical theology," and offers "a new development in Christian language on the resurrection."

95 — Wilks, Michael J. "Roman Empire and the Christian State in the *De civitate Dei.*" *Augustinus* 12 (1967), 489-510.

This essay affirms the influence of Augustine's philosophical dualism on his political theory. Though the author acknowledges "evidence that Augustine recognized the lay power as an institution which had a value in its own right" he sees Augustine deliberately avoiding imperial Rome "even in its Christian form."

Platonic teleology underlies all of Augustine's thought in that the matter of the ultimate, transcendent end is always to be considered. The essay examines the significance of *iustitia* and the Ciceronian *res publica* for Augustine but maintains that the Empire must necessarily be seen from the Christian rather than the Roman perspective. And when Augustine discusses the "two kingdoms" he refers not to church and state but to Christian and non-Christian communities.

So too is there a duality in Augustine's concept of nature — on the one hand divine nature as the result of creation, on the other nature opposed to divinity as a result of the fall. Governmental institutions, the product of secular nature and limited to the temporal sphere, can provide no means of attaining goodness or of preventing the lure of the flesh. The representatives of divinity then must logically exercise influence over the lay members of society. But between them there is no equality, merely a functional cooperative relationship. Finally, while Augustine saw no reason that the Roman administration might not resurface, the study proposes that "Augustine seemed to be envisaging a Christian society of many kingdoms rather than a technically universal empire."

Writings by Augustine

The standard work on the chronology of Augustine's writings is that of S. Zarb, *Chronologia operum sancti Augustini* (Rome: Pontificium Institutum "Angelicum," 1934). See also, E. Lamirande, "Un siecle et demi d'etudes sur l'ecclesiologie de S. Augustin." *Revue des études augustiniennes* 8 (1962), pp. 1-124; A. M. LaBonnardiere, *Recherches de chronologie augustinienne* (Paris: Etudes augustiniennes, 1965).

Latin texts may be found in the following series. *Sancti Aurelii Augustini, opera omnia. Patrologia Latina* (PL). General editor J. P. Migne. Vols. 32-47. Paris, 1841-1845. Also, *Corpus Scriptorum Ecclesiasticorum Latinorum* (CSEL), Vienna, 1899 −; *Corpus Christianorum, Series Latina* (CCSL), The Hague, Nijhoff, 1953 −; and *Bibliotheque Augustinienne* (BA), Paris, 1947 −.

A.D.

386   *Contra academicos* (*Against the Academics*)

386   *De beata vita* (*The Happy Life*)

386   *De ordine* (*On Order*)

386/87   *Soliloquia* (*Soliloquies*)

386/430   *Epistulae* (*Letters*)

387   *De dialectica* (*Logic*), *De grammatica* (*Grammar*)

387   *De immortalitate animae* (*The Immortality of the Soul*)

387/88   *De quantitate animae* (*The Magnitude of the Soul*)

387/89   *De moribus ecclesiae catholicae et de moribus Manichaeorum* (*The Customs of the Catholic Church and the Customs of the Manichees*)

387/90   *De musica* (*On Music*)

388/89   *De genesi contra Manichaeos* (*Commentary on Genesis against the Manichees*)

401   *De opere monachorum (The Work of Monks)*

401   *De sancta virginitate (Holy Virginity)*

401/5   *Contra litteras Petiliani Donatistae (Against the Letters of Petilian the Donatist)*

401/14   *De genesi ad litteram (Literal Commentary on Genesis)*

405   *Epistula ad catholicos de secta donatistarum seu de unitate Ecclesiae (To the Donatists on the Unity of the Church)*

405/6   *Contra Cresconium grammaticum (Against Cresconius the Grammarian)*

406/8   *Contra Donatistam nescio quem (Against an Unknown Donatist)*

406/8   *De divinatione daemonum (On the Prophecies of Demons)*

406/8   *Probationum et testimoniorum contra Donatistas (Proofs and Testimonies Against the Donatists)*

406/9   *Quaestiones 6 expositae contra paganos (Explanation of Six Questions Against the Pagans)*

410   *Epistulae ad Dioscorum (Letter to Dioscorus)*

410   *De urbis excidio (The Fall of Rome)*

411   *De peccatorum meritis et remissione (The Guilt and Remission of Sins)*

411   *De unico baptismo contra Petilianum (On Single Baptism against Petilian)*

411   *Gesta collationis Carthaginiensis (Proceedings of the Conference of Carthage)*

412   *Breviculus collationis cum Donatistis (Summary of the Conference with the Donatists)*

412   *De gratia Testamenti novi (The Grace of the New Testament)*

412   *De maximianistis contra donatistas (On the Maximianists Against the Donatists)*

412   *De spiritu et littera (The Spirit and the Letter)*

413   *Ad Donatistas post collationem (To the Donatists after the Conference)*

413   *Commonitorium ad Fortunatianum (Admonition to Fortunatianus)*

413   *De fide et operibus (Faith and Works)*

413   *De videndo Deo (Letter on the Vision of God)*

413   *In epistulam Iohannis ad Parthos (On the Epistle of John to the Parthians)*

413/15   *De natura et gratia (On Nature and Grace)*

413/18   *Tractatus in evangelium Iohannis CXXIV (Treatises on the Gospel of John)*

413/26   *De civitate Dei (The City of God)*

414   *De bono viduitatis (The Good of Widowhood)*

415   *Ad Orosium contra Priscillianistas et Origenistas (To Orosius against the Priscillianists and Origenists)*

415   *De origine animae (On the Origin of the Soul)*

415   *De perfectione iustitiae hominis (The Perfection of Justice in Man)*

415   *De sententia Iacobi (James' View on the Soul's Origin)*

416   *Ad Emeritum donatistam post collationem (To Emeritus the Donatist After the Conference)*

417   *De correctione Donatistarum (The Correction of the Donatists)*

417   *De gestis Pelagii (The Proceedings against Pelagius)*

417   *De praesentia Dei (The Presence of God)*

418   *De gestis cum Emerito Donatistarum episcopo Caesareae (Debate with Emeritus Donatist Bishop of Caesarea)*

418   *De gratia Christi et de peccato originali (The Grace of Christ and Original Sin)*

418   *De patientia (On Patience in the Face of Suffering)*

418   *Sermo ad Caesariensis Ecclesiae plebem (Sermon for the People of the Church of Caesarea)*

419   *Contra sermonem Arianorum (Against an Arian Sermon)*

429   *De praedestinatione sanctorum (The Predestination of the Blessed)*

429/30   *Adversus Iudaeos (Against the Jews)*

429/30   *Opus imperfectum contra Iulianum (Unfinished Work against Julian)*

Selected General Bibliography

Titles cited in the present study are not included here. The literature on Augustine and his writing is voluminous. For further bibliography the following works should be consulted. *Augustinus-Lexikon*. Stuttgart: Schwabe, 1985 —. *Fichier Augustinien*. Boston: G. K. Hall, 1972 —. *Revue des études augustiniennes*. Paris, 1956 —.

Abercrombie, Nigel. *Saint Augustine and French Classical Thought*. Oxford: Clarendon, 1938. Ch. 2, "Montaigne and the *City of God*."

Alexander, William M. "Sex and Philosophy in Augustine." *Augustinian Studies* 5 (1974), 197-208.

Alfraic, Prosper. *L'évolution intellectuelle de Saint Augustin*. Paris: Nourry, 1918.

Arbesmann, Rudolph. "The Idea of Rome in the Sermons of St. Augustine." *Augustiniana* 4 (1954), 89-108.

Armstrong, A. Hilary. *St. Augustine and Christian Platonism*. Pennsylvania: Villanova University Press, 1967. Rpt. in *Augustine: A Collection of Critical Essays*. New York: Doubleday, 1972. Pp. 3-37.

_____ and Robert A. Markus. *Christian Faith and Greek Philosophy*. London: Darton, Longman, & Todd, 1960.

Arquillière, Henri X. *L'Augustinisme politique. Essai sur la formation des théories politiques du Moyen Age*. Paris: Vrin, 1934. 2nd ed. 1972.

Balmus, C. I. *Étude sur le style de Saint Augustin dans les Confessions et la Cité de Dieu*. Paris: Desclée, 1930.

Bardy, Gustave. *Saint Augustin, l'homme et l'oeuvre*. Paris: Desclée, 1946.

_____. "La formation du concept de 'Cité de Dieu' dans l'oeuvre de saint Augustin." *L'année theologique Augustinienne* 12 (1952), 5-19.

Barrow, Reginald H. *Introduction to St. Augustine, "The City of God."* London: Faber and Faber, 1950.

Battenhouse, Roy W. ed. *A Companion to the Study of Saint Augustine*. New York: Oxford University Press, 1955.

Béné, Charles. *Érasme et Saint Augustin ou l'influence de Saint Augustin sur l'humanisme d'Érasme*. Geneve: Droz, 1969.

Berrouard, M.-F. "S. Augustin et le Ministère de la Prédication." *Recherches augustiniennes* 2 (1961), 447-501.

Bochet, Isabelle. *Saint Augustin et le désir de Dieu*. Paris: *Études augustiniennes*, 1982.

Boler, John. "Augustine and Political Theory." *Mediaevalia: A Journal of Mediaeval Studies* 4(1978), 83-98.

Bonner, Gerald I. *St. Augustine of Hippo: Life and Controversies*. London: Westminster Press, 1963.

_____. *Augustine and Pelagianism in the Light of Modern Research*. Pennsylvania: Villanova University Press, 1972.

_____. "Libido and Concupiscentia in St. Augustine." *Studia Patristica* 3 (1962), 303-314.

_____. "Quid imperatori cum ecclesia? St. Augustine on History and Society." *Augustinian Studies* 2 (1971), 231-251.

Bourke, Vernon J. *Augustine's Quest of Wisdom.* Milwaukee: Bruce, 1945.

_____. *Augustine's View of Reality.* Pennsylvania: Villanova University Press, 1964.

_____. *Joy in Augustine's Ethics.* Pennsylvania: Villanova University Press, 1979.

_____. "Socio-Religious Issues in Augustine's Day." *Augustinian Studies* 4 (1973), 205-212.

_____. "Wisdom in the Gnoseology of St. Augustine." *Augustinus* 3 (1958), 331-336.

_____. "The Political Philosophy of St. Augustine." *Proceedings of the Seventh Annual American Catholic Philosophical Association* 7 (1931), 45-55.

Boyer, Charles. *Christianisme et néo-platonisme dans la formation de S. Augustin.* Paris: Beauchesne, 1920. Rpt. Rome: Libri Catholici, 1953.

_____. *L'idée de vérité dans la philosophie de S. Augustin.* Paris: Beauchesne, 1921.

_____. "La Philosophie Augustinienne ignore-t-elle l'abstraction?" *Nouvelle Revue Théologique* (1930), pp. 1-14.

_____. "La théorie Augustinienne des raisons seminales." In *Essais sur la Doctrine de S. Augustin.* Paris: Beauchesne, 1932. Pp. 97-137.

Brockwell, Charles W. "Augustine's Ideal of Monastic Community: A Paradigm for His Doctrine of the Church." *Augustinian Studies* 8 (1977), 91-109.

Bronson, Larry L. "St. Augustine and Marlowe's Dr. Faustus." *Augustinian Studies* 10 (1979), 19-26.

Brown, Peter. *The World of Late Antiquity.* New York: Harcourt Brace Jovanovich, 1971.

Brown, Peter R. L. "St. Augustine's Attitude to Religious Coercion." *Journal of Roman Studies* 55 (1964), 107-116.

Bubaca, Bruce. *St. Augustine's Theory of Knowledge: A Contemporary Analysis.* New York: Mellen Press, 1981.

Burnaby, John. *Amor Dei: A Study of the Religion of St. Augustine.* London: Hodder and Stoughton, 1938.

_____. "The *Retractions* of St. Augustine: Self-criticism or Apologia?" *Augustinus Magister* 1 (1954), 85-92.

Burrows, Mark S. "Another Look at the Sources of *De Consolatione Philosophiae*: Boethius' Echo of Augustine's Doctrine of 'Providentia.' " *Proceedings of the PMR Conference* 11 (1986), 27-41.

Bushman, Sister Rita Marie. "St. Augustine's Metaphysics and Stoic Doctrine." *New Scholasticism* 26 (1952), 283-304.

Caldwell, Ellen C. "The *loquaces muti* and the *Verbum infans*: Paradox and Language in the *Confessiones* of St. Augustine." In *Collectanea Augustiniana.* New York: Peter Lang, 1990. Pp. 101-111.

Caldwell, Gaylon L. "Augustine's Critique of Human Justice." *A Journal of Church and State* 2 (1960), 7-25.

Callahan, John F. *Augustine and the Greek Philosophers.* Pennsylvania: Villanova University Press, 1967.

Carlyle, R. W. and A. J. Carlyle. *A History of Mediaeval Political Theory in the West.* Vol. 1. *The Second Century to the Ninth.* Edinburgh: Blackwood, 1903-1936. 6 vols.

Caton, Hiram. "St. Augustine's Critique of Politics." *New Scholasticism* 47 (1973), 433-457.

Cayre, Fulbert. "Le sens et l'unité des Confessions de Saint Augustin." *L'année théologique augustinienne* 13 (1953), 13-32.

Chabannes, Jacques. *St. Augustine.* Trans. J. Kernan. New York: Doubleday, 1962.

Chadwick, Henry. *Augustine.* New York: Oxford University Press, 1986.

Chroust, Anton-Hermann. "The Philosophy of Law of St. Augustine." *Philosophical Review* 53 (1944), 195-202.

Clark, Mary T. *Augustine, Philosopher of Freedom. A Study in Comparative Philosophy.* New York: DesClée, 1958.

_____. *Augustinian Personalism.* Pennsylvania: Villanova University Press, 1970.

_____. "Augustine on Justice." *Revue des études augustiniennes* 9 (1963), 87-94.

Cochrane, Charles Norris. *Christianity and Classical Culture: A Study of Thought and Action from Augustus to Augustine.* New York: Oxford University Press, 1942. 2d ed. 1957.

Colbert, Mary C. *The Syntax of the* De Civitate Dei *of St. Augustine.* Washington, D.C.: Catholic University of America Press, 1923.

Combes, Gustave. *La doctrine politique de Saint Augustin.* Paris: Plon, 1927.

Congar, Yves. *L'Ecclésiologie du haut Moyen Age.* Paris: Cerf, 1968.

_____. " 'Civitas Dei' et 'Ecclesia' chez S. Augustin." *Revue des études augustiniennes* 3 (1957), 1-14.

Copleston, Frederick. *History of Philosophy.* Vol. 2. Maryland: Newman Press, 1950. Rpt. New York: Doubleday, 1962.

Coughlan, M. J. " 'Si Fallor, Sum' Revisited." *Augustinian Studies* 13 (1982), 145-150.

Courcelle, Pierre P. *Recherches sur les 'Confessions' de S. Augustin.* Paris: De Boccard, 1950. 2nd ed. 1968.

_____. *Les 'Confessions' de S. Augustin dans la tradition littéraire: antécédents et postérité.* Paris: *Études augustiniennes,* 1963.

Couturier, Charles. "La structure métaphysique de l'homme d'après S. Augustin." *Augustinus Magister* 1 (1954), 543-550.

Cranz, F. Edward. "The Development of Augustine's Ideas on Society Before the Donatist Controversy." *Harvard Theological Review* 47 (1954), 255-316. Rpt. in *Augustine: A Collection of Critical Essays.* Ed. Robert A. Markus. New York: Doubleday, 1972. Pp. 336-403.

Daniels, Donald E. "The Argument of the *De Trinitate* and Augustine's Theory of Signs." *Augustinian Studies* 8 (1977), 33-54.

D'Arcy, Martin C. *The Meaning and Matter of History.* New York: Farrar, Straus, and Cudahy, 1961.

D'Arcy, M. C. "The Philosophy of St. Augustine." In *A Monument to Saint Augustine.* M. C. D'Arcy et al. London: Sheed and Ward, 1930. Pp. 153-195. Rpt. 1945.

_____, et al. *A Monument to Saint Augustine: Essays on Some Aspects of His Thought Written in Commemoration of His 15th Centenary.* London: Sheed and Ward, 1930. Rpt. 1945.

Duval, Yves-Marie. "L'éloge de Théodose dans la Cité de Dieu (V.26.1)." *Recherches augustiniennes* 4 (1966), 135-179.

Dvornik, Francis. *Early Christian and Byzantine Political Philosophy.* Dumbarton Oaks Studies Nine, The Dumbarton Oaks Center for Byzantine Studies, Washington, D. C., 1966, Vol. II.

Evans, Gillian. *Augustine on Evil.* London: Cambridge University Press, 1982.

Ferguson, Margaret W. "Saint Augustine's Region of Unlikeness: the Crossing of Exile and Language." *The Georgia Review* 29 (1976), 842-864.

Finaert, Joseph. *L'évolution littéraire de Saint Augustin.* Collection d'Etudes Latines, 17. Paris: Belles Lettres, 1939.

Fortin, Ernest L. *Christianisme et Culture philosophique au cinquième siècle.* Paris: *Études augustiniennes,* 1959.

_____. "Reflections on the Proper Way to Read Augustine the Theologian." *Augustinian Studies* 2 (1971), 253-272.

_____. "The Political Implications of St. Augustine's Theory of Conscience." *Augustinian Studies* 1 (1972), 133-152.

Frend, W. H. C. *The Donatist Church.* Oxford: Clarendon Press, 1952. Rpt. 1971.

_____. "Manichaeism in the Struggle Between St. Augustine and Petiline of Constantine." *Augustinus Magister* 2 (1954), 859-866.

Friberg, Hans Daniel. *Love and Justice in Political Theory. A Study of Augustine's Definition of the Commonwealth.* Chicago: University of Chicago Press, 1944.

Gannon, Sister M. Ann Ida. "The Active Theory of Sensation in St. Augustine." *New Scholasticism* 30 (1956), 154-180.

Gierke, Otto. *Political Theories of the Middle Ages.* Trans. with intro. by Frederic W. Maitland. Boston: Beacon Press, 1958.

Gilson, Etienne. *L'introduction à l'étude de Saint Augustin.* Paris: Vrin, 1929. Rpt. 1949. Trans. L. E. M. Lynch. *The Christian Philosophy of Saint Augustine.* New York: Knopf, 1960.

——————. "Forward to the *City of God.*" *City of God.* New York: Fathers of the Church, 1950.

——————. *Études sur le rôle de la pensée Médiévale dans la formation du système Cartésien.* Paris: Vrin, 1975.

——————. *Les métamorphoses de la Cité de Dieu.* Paris: Vrin, 1952.

——————. *History of Christian Philosophy in the Middle Ages.* New York: Random House, 1955.

——————. "The Future of Augustinian Metaphysics." In *A Monument to Saint Augustine.* M. C. D'Arcy et al. London: Sheed and Ward, 1930. Pp. 287-315. Rpt. 1945.

Green, William M. "Augustine on the Teaching of History." In *University of California Publications in Classical Philology* 12 (1944), 315-342. Berkeley: University of California Press, 1944.

——————. "Initium omnis peccati superbia: Augustine on Pride as the First Sin." In *University of California Publications in Classical Philology* 13 (1949), 407-431. Berkeley: University of California Press, 1949.

Guardini, Romano. *The Conversion of St. Augustine.* Trans. E. Briefs. Maryland: Newman Press, 1960.

Guitton, Jean. *Le temps et l'éternité chez Plotin et Saint Augustin.* Paris: Boivin, 1933.

Guy, Jean-Claude. *Unité et structure logique de la 'Cité de Dieu' de Saint Augustin.* Paris: Études augustiniennes, 1961.

Hearnshaw, F. J. C., ed. *Social and Political Ideas of Some Great Medieval Thinkers*. London: Harrap, 1923.

Henry, Paul. "Augustine and Plotinus." *Journal of Theological Studies* 38 (1937), 1-23.

Hohensee, H. *The Augustinian Concept of Authority*. New York: Paulist Press, 1954.

Holscher, Ludger. *The Reality of the Mind: Augustine's Philosophical Arguments for the Human Soul as a Spiritual Substance*. London: Routledge and Kegan Paul, 1986.

Holte, Ragnar. *Béatitude et sagesse: S. Augustin et le problème de la fin de l'homme dans la philosophie ancienne*. Paris: *Études augustiniennes*,1962.

Huftier, Maurice. *Le Tragique de la Condition Chrétienne chez Saint Augustin*. Paris: Desclée, 1964.

Hultgren, Gunnar. *Le Commandement d'amour chez Augustin. Interprétation philosophique et théologique d'après les écrits de la periode 386-400*. Paris: Vrin, 1939.

Jacquin, Armand-Pierre. "La prédestination d'après S. Augustin." *Miscellanea Agostiniana* 2 (1931), 855-868.

Kaufmann, N. "Les eléments Aristotéliens dans la cosmologie et la psychologie de S. Augustin." *Revue Néoscholastique de Philosophie* 11 (1904), 140-156.

Keenan, M. Emily. *The Life and Times of St. Augustine as Revealed in His Letters*. Washington: Catholic University of America, 1935.

Kevane, Eugene. "Augustine's Christian Paideia." *Augustinian Studies* 1 (1970), 154-180.

Keyes, Gordon L. *Christian Faith and the Interpretation of History: A Study of St. Augustine's Philosophy of History.* Nebraska: University of Nebraska Press, 1966.

Klegeman, C. "A Psychoanalytic Study of the Confessions of St. Augustine." *Journal of the American Psychoanalytic Association* 5 (1957), 469-484.

Lambot, Cyrille. "Lettre inédite de Saint Augustin relative au *De Civitate Dei.*" *Revue Benedictine* 51 (1939), 109-121.

Lamirande, Emilien. *Church, State, and Toleration. An Intriguing Change of Mind in St. Augustine.* Pennsylvania: Villanova University Press, 1974.

Lamotte, J. "But et adversaires de saint Augustin dans le 'De Civitate Dei.'" *Augustiniana* 11 (1961), 434-469.

Lauras, A. and H. Rondet. "Le thème des deux cites dans l'oeuvre de s. Augustin." *Études augustiniennes* (1953), 99-160.

Lawless, George P. *Augustine of Hippo and His Monastic Rule.* New York: Oxford University Press, 1987.

_____. "Interior Peace in the *Confessions* of St. Augustine." *Revue des études augustiniennes* 26 (1980), 45-61.

Limbrick, Elaine. "Montaigne et Saint Augustine." *Bibliothèque d'Humanisme et Renaissance* 34 (1972), 49-64.

McElwain, Hugh T. *St. Augustine's Doctrine on War in Relation to Earlier Ecclesiastial Writers (A Comparative Analysis).* Chicago: Regnery, 1973.

MacQueen, D. J. "St. Augustine's Concept of Property Ownership." *Recherches augustiniennes* 8 (1972), 187-229.

Maritain, Jacques. "St. Augustine and St. Thomas Aquinas." In *A Monument to Saint Augustine.* M. C. D'Arcy et al. London: Sheed and Ward, 1930. Pp. 197-223. Rpt. 1945.

Markus, Robert A. *Conversion and Disenchantment in Augustine's Spiritual Career.* Pennsylvania: Villanova University Press, 1986.

_____. "The Roman Empire in Early Christian Historiography." *Downside Review* 81 (1963), 340-354.

_____. " 'Imago' and 'Similitudo' in Augustine." *Revue des études augustiniennes* 11 (1964), 125-143.

_____. *"Alienatio*: Philosophy and Eschatology in the Development of an Augustinian Idea." *Studia Patristica* 9 (1966), 431-450.

_____. ed. *Augustine: A Collection of Critical Essays.* New York: Doubleday, 1972.

Marrou, Henri-Irénée. *S. Augustin et la fin de la culture antique.* Paris: DeBoccard, 1938. Rpt. 1949.

_____. *L'Ambivalence du temps de l'histoire chez S. Augustin.* Paris: Vrin, 1950.

_____. *St. Augustine and His Influence Through the Ages.* London: Longmans, 1957.

_____. *The Resurrection and Saint Augustine's Theology of Human Values.* Pennsylvania: Villanova University Press, 1966.

_____. *Time and Timelessness.* New York: Sheed and Ward, 1969.

_____. "La Division en Chapitres des Livres de la 'Cité de Dieu.' " *Melanges J. de Ghellinck* 1 (1951), 235-249.

_____. "Civitas Dei, Civitas Terrena: num tertium quid?" *Studia Patristica* 2 (1957), 342-350.

_____. "Un Lieu dit 'Cité de Dieu.' " *Augustinus Magister* 1 (1954), 101-110.

_____ and Anne Marie La Bonnardiere. "Le Dogme de la Résurrection et la Théologie des Valeurs Humains selon l'Enseignement de Saint Augustin." *Revue des études augustiniennes* 12 (1966), 111-136. Trans. *The Resurrection and Saint Augustine's Theology of Human Values.* Pennsylvania: Villanova University Press, 1966.

Mazzeo, Joseph A. "Saint Augustine's Rhetoric of Silence: Truth versus Eloquence and Things versus Signs." In *Renaissance and Seventeenth-Century Studies.* New York: Columbia University Press, 1964. Pp. 1-28.

Meagher, Robert E. *An Introduction to Augustine.* New York: New York University Press, 1978.

Miethe, Terry L. "St. Augustine and Sense Knowledge." *Augustinian Studies* 8 (1977), 11-19.

Miles, Margaret R. *St. Augustine's Idea of the Meaning and Value of the Body in Relation to the Whole Personality.* California: Graduate Theological Union Dissertation, 1977.

Monagle, John F. "Friendship in St. Augustine's Biography." *Augustinian Studies* 2 (1971), pp. 81-92.

Morgan, James. *The Psychological Teaching of St. Augustine.* London: Elliot Stock, 1932.

Morrison, John L. "Augustine's Two Theories of Time." *New Scholasticism* 45 (1971), 600-610.

Mourant, John A. *Introduction to the Philosophy of St. Augustine.* Pennsylvania: Pennsylvania State University Press, 1964.

_____. *Augustine on Immortality.* Pennsylvania: Villanova University Press, 1969.

_____. *St. Augustine on Memory*. Pennsylvania: Villanova University Press, 1980.

_____. "The Emergence of a Christian Philosophy in the Dialogues of St. Augustine." *Augustinian Studies* 1 (1970), 70-88.

_____. "Augustine on Miracles." *Augustinian Studies* 4 (1973), 103-127.

Newton, John T. "The Importance of Augustine's Use of the Neoplatonic Doctrine of Hypostatic Union for the Development of Christology." *Augustinian Studies* 2 (1971), 1-16.

Niebuhr, Reinhold. "Augustine's Political Realism." In *Christian Realism and Political Problems*. New York: Scribner, 1953.

O'Brien, William J. "Original Sin in Augustine's 'Confessions'." *Thought* 49 (1974), 436-446.

O'Connell, Robert J. *St. Augustine's Early Theory of Man, A.D. 386-391*. Massachusetts: Harvard University Press, 1968.

_____. *Saint Augustine's Confessions: The Odyssey of the Soul*. Massachusetts: Harvard University Press, 1969.

_____. *Saint Augustine's Platonism*. Pennsylvania: Villanova University Press, 1984.

_____. *Imagination and Metaphysics in St. Augustine*. Milwaukee: Marquette University Press, 1986.

_____. "Augustine's Rejection of the Fall of the Soul." *Augustinian Studies* 4 (1973), 1-32.

_____. "The Riddle of Augustine's *Confessions*: A Plotinian Key." *International Philosophical Quarterly* 4 (1964), 327-372.

_____. "*Ennead* VI, 4 and 5 in the Works of St. Augustine." *Revue des études augustiniennes* 9 (1963), 1-39.

_____. "The *Ennead* and St. Augustine's Image of Happiness." *Vigiliae Christianae* 17 (1963), 129-164.

_____. "The Plotinian Fall of the Soul in St. Augustine." *Traditio* 19 (1963), 1-35.

O'Daly, Gerard J. P. "Augustine on the Measurement of Time: Some Comparisons with Aristotelian and Stoic Texts." In *Neoplatonism and Early Christian Thought.* Ed. Henry J. Blumenthal and Robert A. Markus. London: Variorum Publications, 1981. Pp. 171-179.

O'Donovan, Oliver. *The Problem of Self-Love in St. Augustine.* New Haven: Yale University Press, 1980.

O'Dowd, W.B. "Development of Augustine's Opinions on Religious Toleration." *Irish Theological Quarterly* (1919), 337-348.

O'Meara, John J. *The Creation of Man in St. Augustine's* De Genesi ad Litteram. Pennsylvania: Villanova University Press, 1977.

_____. *The Young Augustine: The Growth of St. Augustine's Mind up to His Conversion.* London: Longmans, 1954.

_____. *Porphyry's Philosophy from Oracles in Augustine.* Paris: *Études augustiniennes,* 1959.

_____, ed. *An Augustine Reader.* New York: Image Books, 1973.

_____. "The Platonist Augustinian Inheritance of St. Thomas." *Irish Theological Quarterly* 41 (1974), 312-316.

_____. "St. Augustine's Attitude to Love." *Arethusa* 2 (1969), 46-60.

_____. "Augustine the Artist and the *Aeneid*." In "Mélanges offerts à Mlle. Christine Mohrmann." *Spectrum* (1963), 252-261.

_____. "Augustine and Neo-Platonism." *Recherches augustiniennes* 1 (1958), 91-111.

_____. "The Historicity of the Early Dialogues of Saint Augustine." *Vigiliae Christianae* 5 (1951), 150-178.

O'Toole, Christopher J. *The Philosophy of Creation in the Writings of St. Augustine.* Washington: The Catholic University of America Press, 1944.

Paolini, Shirley J. *Confessions of Sin and Love in the Middle Ages: Dante's* Commedia *and St. Augustine's* Confessions. Washington, D.C.: University Press of America, 1982.

Paolucci, Henry, ed. *The Political Writings of St. Augustine.* Chicago: Regnery Co., 1962.

Papini, Giovanni. *St. Augustine.* Paris: Plon, 1930.

Pegis, Anton C. "The Mind of St. Augustine." *Medieval Studies* 6 (1944), 1-61.

Pelikan, Jaroslav J. *The Christian Tradition: A History of the Development of Doctrine. Vol. 1, The Emergence of the Catholic Tradition (100-600).* Chicago: University of Chicago Press, 1971.

_____. *The Mystery of Continuity: Time and History, Memory and Eternity in the Thought of St. Augustine.* Charlottesville: University Press of Virginia, 1986.

Pepin, Jean. *Saint Augustine et la Dialectique.* Pennsylvania: Villanova University Press, 1976.

Pincherle, Alberto. "The Confessions of St. Augustine: A Reappraisal." *Augustinian Studies* 7 (1976), 119-133.

Pope, Hugh. *St. Augustine of Hippo*. Maryland: Newman Press, 1949. Rpt. New York: Doubleday, 1961.

Portalié, Eugène. *A Guide to the Thought of St. Augustine*. Trans. R. J. Bastian. Chicago: Regnery, 1960.

Preus, Mary C. *Eloquence and Ignorance in Augustine's* On the Nature and Origin of the Soul. Georgia: Scholars Press, 1985.

Przywara, Erich. "St. Augustine and the Modern World." In *A Monument to Saint Augustine*. M. C. D'Arcy et al. London: Sheed and Ward, 1930. Pp. 249-286. Rpt. 1945.

Quinn, John M. *Praise in St. Augustine: Readings and Reflections*. Massachusetts: Christopher Publishing House, 1987.

_____. "Four Faces of Time in St. Augustine." Scheduled for publication in *Recherches augustiniennes* 26 (1992).

_____. "Anti-Manichean and Other Moral Precisions in Augustine's Confessions." *Augustinian Studies* 19 (1988).

_____. "Augustine's View of Reality." *Augustinianum* 8 (1968), 140-146.

Ramsey, Paul. *War and the Christian Conscience*. North Carolina: Duke University Press, 1961.

Reeves, John-Baptist. "St. Augustine and Humanism." In *A Monument to Saint Augustine*. M. C. D'Arcy et al. London: Sheed and Ward, 1930. Pp. 121-151. Rpt. 1945.

Renna, Thomas. "Augustinian Autobiography: Medieval and Modern." *Augustinian Studies* 11 (1980), 197-204.

_____. "The Idea of Peace in the Augustinian Tradition." *Augustinian Studies* 10 (1979), 105-111.

Riley, George F. *The Role of Marcus Tullius Cicero in the Educational Formation of St. Augustine of Hippo.* Washington: Catholic University of America, 1969.

Rist, John M. "Augustine on Free Will and Predestination." *Journal of Theological Studies* 29 (1969), 420-427. Rpt. in *Augustine: A Collection of Critical Essays.* Ed. Robert A. Markus. New York: Doubleday, 1972. Pp. 218-252.

Roche, W. J. "Measure, Number and Weight in St. Augustine." *New Scholasticism* 15 (1941), 350-376.

Rohmer, Jean. *La finalité morale de Saint Augustin à Duns Scot.* Paris: Vrin, 1939.

Rondet, Henri. *Essais sur la théologie de la grâce.* Paris: 1964.

Rowe, Trevor T. *St. Augustine, Pastoral Theologian.* London: Epworth Press, 1974.

Ryan, John K. "Augustinian Doctrine of Peace and War." *American Ecclesiastical Review* (1947), 401-421.

Schmidt, Mary T. *St. Augustine's Influence on St. Thomas More's English Works.* Connecticut: Yale University Dissertation, 1943.

Schnaubelt, Joseph C., O.S.A. and Frederick Van Fleteren, eds. *Collectanea Augustiniana.* New York: Peter Lang, 1990.

Sherwin-White, Adrien N. *The Roman Citizenship.* Oxford: Clarendon, 1973.

Shinn, Roger. "Augustinian and Cyclical Views of History." *Anglican Theological Review* 131 (1949), 133-141.

Stark, Judith Chelius. "The Dynamics of the Will in Augustine's Conversion." In *Collectanea Augustiniana.* New York: Peter Lang, 1990. Pp. 45-64.

Sticca, Sandro. "The Augustinian Tradition in the Middle Ages." *Mediaevalia: A Journal of Mediaeval Studies* 4 (1978), 1-12.

Straw, Carole E. "Augustine as Pastoral Theologian: The Exegesis of the Parables of the Field and Threshing Floor." *Augustinian Studies* 14 (1983), 129-151.

Suchocki, Marjorie. "The Symbolic Structure of Augustine's *Confessions.*" *Journal of the American Academy of Religion* 3 (1980), 365-378.

Suter, Ronald. "Augustine on Time With Some Criticisms from Wittgenstein." *Revue internationale de philosophie* 16 (1962), 378-394.

TeSelle, Eugene. *Augustine the Theologian.* New York: Herder, 1970.

_____. *Augustine's Strategy as an Apologist.* Pennsylvania: Villanova University Press, 1974.

_____. "Porphyry and Augustine." *Augustinian Studies* 5 (1974), 113-148.

_____. "Some Reflections on Augustine's Use of Scripture." *Augustinian Studies* 7 (1976), 165-178.

Testard, Maurice. *Saint Augustin et Ciceron.* Vol. I. *Ciceron dans la formation et dans l'oeuvre de Saint Augustin.* Paris: *Études augustiniennes*, 1958. 2 vols.

Thonnard, F.-J. "La Predestination Augustinienne. Sa Place en Philosophie Augustinienne." *Revue des études augustiniennes* 10 (1964), 97-123.

Thundy, Zacharius P. "Love: Augustine and Chaucer." *Augustinian Studies* 14 (1983), 93-103.

Van der Meer, Frederick. *Augustine the Bishop: Religion and Society at the Dawn of the Middle Ages.* Trans. B. Battershaw and G. R. Lamb. New York: Harper and Row, 1965.

Van Fleteren, Frederick. "St. Augustine's Theory of Conversion." In *Collectanea Augustiniana*. New York: Peter Lang, 1990. Pp. 65-80.

_____. "Authority and Reason, Faith and Understanding in the Thought of St. Augustine." *Augustinian Studies* 4 (1973), 33-71.

_____. "Erasmus and Augustine. A Comment on a Recent Work." *Augustinian Studies* 3 (1972), 191-205.

Verheijen, Luc. *St. Augustine's Monasticism in the Light of Acts 4:32-35*. Pennsylvania: Villanova University Press, 1979.

Von Jess, Wilma G. "Augustine: A Consistent and Unitary Theory of Time." *New Scholasticism* 46 (1972), 337-351.

Watkin, E. I. "The Mysticism of Saint Augustine." In *A Monument to Saint Augustine*. M. C. D'Arcy et al. London: Sheed and Ward, 1930. Pp. 103-119. Rpt. 1945.

West, Rebecca. *St. Augustine*. New York: Appleton, 1933.

Wilks, Michael J. "Augustine and the General Will," *Studia Patristica* 9 (1966), 487-522.

Willis, Geoffrey G. *St. Augustine and the Donatist Controversy*. London: S.P.C.K., 1950.

Wilson-Kastner, Patricia. "Andreas Osiander's Theology of Grace in the Perspective of the Influence of Augustine of Hippo." *Sixteenth Century Journal* 10 (1979), 72-91.

_____. "Grace as Participation in the Divine Life in the Theology of Augustine of Hippo; Augustine's Relationship to the Greek Theological World in Respect to the Question of Grace." *Augustinian Studies* 7 (1976), 135-152.